CHAPTER 5

Resource Book

The Resource Book contains a wide variety of blackline masters available for Chapter 5. The blacklines are organized by lesson. Included are support materials for the teacher as well as practice, activities, applications, and project resources.

McDougal Littell
A HOUGHTON MIFFLIN COMPANY
Evanston, Illinois • Boston • Dallas

Contributing Authors

The authors wish to thank the following individuals for their contributions to the Chapter 5 Resource Book.

Christine Cox
Donna Foley
Rebecca Salmon Glus
Julie Groth
Mark Johnson
Michelle McCarney
Leslie Palmer
Jessica Pflueger
Donna Rose
Monica Single

ISBN: 0-618-26887-1

123456789–BHV–07 06 05 04 03

Contents

Variables and Equations

Contents

Contents

Descriptions of Resources

This Chapter Resource Book is organized by lessons within the chapter in order to make your planning easier. The following materials are provided:

Tips for New Teachers These teaching notes provide both new and experienced teachers with useful teaching tips for each lesson, including tips about common errors and inclusion.

Parents as Partners This guide helps parents contribute to student success by providing an overview of the chapter along with questions and activities for parents and students to work on together.

Lesson Plans and Lesson Plans for Block Scheduling This planning template helps teachers select the materials they will use to teach each lesson from among the variety of materials available for the lesson. The block-scheduling version provides additional information about pacing.

Activity Support Masters These blackline masters make it easier for students to record their work on selected activities in the Student Edition.

Technology Activities with Keystrokes Keystrokes for various models of calculators are provided for each Technology Activity in the Student Edition where appropriate, along with alternative Technology Activities for selected lessons.

Practice A, B, and C These exercises offer additional practice for the material in each lesson, including application problems. There are three levels of practice for each lesson: A (basic), B (average), and C (advanced).

Study Guide These two pages provide additional instruction, worked-out examples, and practice exercises covering the key concepts and vocabulary in each lesson.

Real-World Problem Solving These exercises offer problem-solving activities for the material in selected lessons in a real world context.

Challenge Practice These exercises offer challenging practice on the mathematics of each lesson for advanced students.

Chapter Review Games and Activities This worksheet offers fun practice at the end of the chapter and provides an alternative way to review the chapter content in preparation for the Chapter Test.

Projects with Rubric These projects allow students to delve more deeply into a problem that applies the mathematics of the chapter. Teacher's notes and a 4-point rubric are included. The projects include a real-life project, a cooperative project, and an independent extra credit project.

Cumulative Practice These practice pages help students maintain skills from the current chapter and preceding chapters.

CHAPTER 5

Tips for New Teachers

For use with Chapter 5

Lesson 5.1

COMMON ERROR One basic, common error students make when adding fractions is to add the denominators. Begin with the diagram at the top of page 219. Be sure that students understand that the denominator, 5, represents the *size* of the pieces, not the *number* of shaded pieces. Numbers get added, not sizes.

TEACHING TIP Be sure to discuss the Notebook box on page 219, especially the Algebra entry. Sometimes seeing the addition and subtraction of algebraic fractions can help students to remember the procedures for numerical fractions.

COMMON ERROR Be sure that students understand the following relationships:

$$-\frac{a}{b} = \frac{-a}{b} = \frac{a}{-b} \text{ and } \frac{a}{b} = \frac{-a}{-b}$$

$a = 1a$ and $-a = -1a$

TEACHING TIP Some students may be more successful using a vertical format to subtract mixed numbers requiring renaming. You may wish to demonstrate this format using Example 1b.

Lesson 5.2

TEACHING TIP When adding a positive fraction and a negative fraction with unlike denominators, it is, of course, necessary to determine the fraction with the larger absolute value to find the sign of the sum. Some students may try to determine the sign before finding a common denominator and writing equivalent fractions. They should be dissuaded from doing so as it will be easier to compare absolute values after the fractions are rewritten over the common denominator.

COMMON ERROR In Example 2b on page 225, some students may wish to incorrectly simplify the fraction $\frac{40 + 7y}{8y}$ by using a factor of 8 or a factor of y. Show students that, in order to simplify, a number must be a factor of the *entire* numerator or denominator, not just of a term in either one. If necessary, have students choose a value to substitute for y and then evaluate the original expression and the incorrectly simplified expression to further convince themselves of the error.

INCLUSION Operations with fractions often require many steps that must be done in a specified order. Be sure to provide several models and even reference cards for students who may have difficulty in remembering and sequencing the necessary steps.

Problem Solving Strategies 5.3

INCLUSION You may wish to have students complete this lesson in carefully chosen cooperative groups so that all students may have access to this problem solving strategy.

Lesson 5.3

COMMON ERROR Remind students that they need to find common denominators only for adding, subtracting, and comparing fractions, not for multiplying or dividing fractions.

COMMON ERROR Be aware of students who, when multiplying mixed numbers, may multiply the whole numbers together and then the fractions together. Remind those students to convert the mixed numbers into improper fractions before multiplying.

COMMON ERROR To help students convert negative mixed numbers into fractions, provide the following example:

$$-4\frac{5}{6} = -\left(4\frac{5}{6}\right) = -\left(\frac{29}{6}\right) = -\frac{29}{6}$$

CHAPTER 5 Continued

Tips for New Teachers

For use with Chapter 5

Lesson 5.4

TEACHING TIP Be sure to reinforce vocabulary terms such as *reciprocal* and *multiplicative inverse.*

COMMON ERROR To help students to remember to take *only* the reciprocal of the divisor, remind them that the first number (the dividend) in a division expression is the "starting point" and the second number (the divisor) is the "operator". Also, remind students that common factors may be canceled only when *multiplying* fractions, *not* when dividing. Thus, students must take the reciprocal of the divisor before canceling common factors.

TEACHING TIP When multiplying or dividing negative fractions, encourage students to determine and *write* the sign of the answer *first.* Often students forget to do this after performing the required algorithm.

Technology Activity 5.4

TEACHING TIP Many calculators handle fractions differently or not at all. Unless you have a classroom set of calculators, be prepared to help students individually to become proficient on their own personal calculators.

Lesson 5.5

TEACHING TIP If students understand that the root word of *rational* is *ratio*, it can help them to identify rational (and later irrational) numbers.

TEACHING TIP In Example 2 on page 243, if students are having difficulty comparing decimal numbers, remind them to add zeroes to the right of the number so that all the decimal parts have the same number of digits. This way they can compare numbers written to the same place value.

TEACHING TIP Writing terminating decimals as fractions is easier if students read decimals using place value (*thirty-five hundredths* as opposed to *point three five*).

Lesson 5.6

TEACHING TIP While doing Example 1b, stress the importance of using 0 as a place holder when adding and, especially, subtracting fractions.

Lesson 5.7

TEACHING TIP Be sure to give examples of multiplication of decimals where the two factors have a different number of decimal places. Have students note that the decimal points need to align only for addition and subtraction, not for multiplication.

Hands-on Activity 5.8

TEACHING TIP You may wish to pool the data collected from all groups to get a more accurate mean, median, and mode.

Lesson 5.8

TEACHING TIP Exercises 16-18 on page 260 are a good assessment of students' understanding of mean, median, and mode.

CHAPTER 5

Name ______________________________ Date __________

Parents as Partners

For use with Chapter 5

Chapter Overview One way you can help your student succeed in Chapter 5 is by discussing the lesson goals in the chart below. When a lesson is completed, ask your student the following questions. "What were the goals of the lesson? What new words and formulas did you learn? How can you apply the ideas of the lesson to your life?"

Lesson Title	*Lesson Goals*	*Key Applications*
5.1: Fractions with Common Denominators	Add and subtract fractions with common denominators.	• Corn Snake • Knitting • Euros • Auto Racing
5.2: Fractions with Different Denominators	Add and subtract fractions with different denominators.	• Carpentry • Canoeing • Sledding • Equator
5.3: Multiplying Fractions	Multiply fractions and mixed numbers.	• Postcards • Snack Mix • Moon Craters
5.4: Dividing Fractions	Divide fractions.	• Photography • Dog Food • CD Player
5.5: Fractions and Decimals	Write fractions as decimals and decimals as fractions. Order rational numbers.	• Finches • Stock Listings • Breakfast Foods
5.6: Adding and Subtracting Decimals	Add and subtract decimals. Use front-end estimation.	• Dancing • Theater Supplies • Track Times • Banking
5.7: Multiplying and Dividing Decimals	Multiply and divide decimals.	• Rafting • Balloons • Lava Flows
5.8: Mean, Median, and Mode	Describe data sets using mean, median, mode, and range. Choose a representative average.	• Deep Sea Jellies • Ice Cream • Gymnastics • Bowling

Know How to Take Notes

Writing Helpful Hints is the strategy featured in Chapter 5 (see page 218). Your student should record any helpful hints for solving problems that either the teacher or the textbook mentions. Check to see that your student has recorded the hints for subtracting mixed numbers that are found in Lesson 5.1. Your student should record any personalized hints or reminders as well.

Name ______________________ Date ________

Parents as Partners

For use with Chapter 5

Key Ideas Your student can demonstrate understanding of key concepts by working through the following exercises with you.

Lesson	*Exercise*
5.1	Carmen had miniature train tracks that were $71\frac{1}{4}$ inches long. He added $42\frac{3}{4}$ inches of track to them. How much track does he now have?
5.2	Your family is purchasing a new refrigerator. You have a space that is $33\frac{11}{16}$ inches wide for it to fit into. You find a refrigerator that is $31\frac{3}{8}$ inches wide. How much width is left over?
5.3	Camryn has a string of 193 paper clips. Each paper clip is $1\frac{5}{16}$ inches. How long is her string of paper clips?
5.4	The keyboard of a piano is $45\frac{1}{2}$ inches long. Each white piano key is $\frac{7}{8}$ inch wide. How many white keys are there on the piano?
5.5	Order the numbers from least to greatest. $1\frac{5}{8}$, $1\frac{7}{16}$, 1.79, $1\frac{1}{3}$, 1.5
5.6	You found a poster for \$7.49. You used a coupon for \$1.50 off when you purchased the poster. How much did you pay?
5.7	A penny is 1.9 centimeters across. (a) If 325 pennies were placed side-by-side, how long would the line of pennies be? (b) A line of pennies is 110.2 centimeters long. How many pennies are there?
5.8	Find the mean, median, mode(s), and range of the prices below. \$1.41, \$1.39, \$1.54, \$1.39, \$1.44, \$1.33, \$1.51, \$1.33

Home Involvement Activity

Directions: Record the daily amount of precipitation (rain or snow) that falls for the next month. Find the mean, median, mode(s) and range of precipitation for the month. If the months' averages were the same throughout the year, how much total precipitation would your area receive each year based on each average? You can also compare your findings to those in other areas, ordering your findings from least to greatest.

Answers

5.1: 114 in. **5.2:** $2\frac{5}{16}$ in. **5.3:** $253\frac{5}{16}$ in. **5.4:** 52 **5.5:** $1\frac{1}{3}$, $1\frac{7}{16}$, 1.5, $1\frac{5}{8}$, 1.79
5.6: \$5.99 **5.7: a.** 617.5 cm **b.** 58 **5.8:** mean: \$1.4175; median: \$1.40;
modes: \$1.33, \$1.39; range: \$.21

Teacher's Name ______________________ Class ______ Room ______ Date ______

Lesson Plan

1-day lesson (See *Pacing and Assignment Guide*, TE page 216A)

For use with pages 219–223

GOAL **Add and subtract fractions with common denominators.**

State/Local Objectives ____

____

✓ Check the items you wish to use for this lesson.

STARTING OPTIONS

____ Warm-Up: Transparencies

TEACHING OPTIONS

____ Notetaking Guide
____ Examples: 1–4, SE pages 219–221
____ Extra Examples: TE pages 220–221
____ Your Turn Now Exercises: 1–7, SE pages 220–221
____ Concept Check: TE page 221
____ Getting Ready to Practice Exercises: 1–11, SE page 221

APPLY/HOMEWORK

Homework Assignment

____ Basic: SRH p. 710 Exs. 6–10; pp. 222–223 Exs. 12–28, 31–36, 41, 47–63
____ Average: pp. 222–223 Exs. 16–30, 34–44, 49–64
____ Advanced: pp. 222–223 Exs. 20–30, 37–58*, 62–64

Reteaching the Lesson

____ Practice: CRB pages 7–9 (Level A, Level B, Level C); Practice Workbook
____ Study Guide: CRB pages 10–11; Spanish Study Guide

Extending the Lesson

____ Challenge: SE page 223; CRB page 12

ASSESSMENT OPTIONS

____ Daily Quiz (5.1): TE page 223 or Transparencies
____ Test-Taking Practice: SE page 223

Notes ____

____

____

LESSON 5.1

Teacher's Name ____________ Class ______ Room ______ Date ______

Lesson Plan for Block Scheduling

Half-block lesson (See *Pacing and Assignment Guide*, TE page 216A)

For use with pages 219–223

GOAL **Add and subtract fractions with common denominators.**

State/Local Objectives ____________

____

✓ Check the items you wish to use for this lesson.

STARTING OPTIONS

____ Warm-Up: Transparencies

TEACHING OPTIONS

____ Notetaking Guide
____ Examples: 1–4, SE pages 219–221
____ Extra Examples: TE pages 220–221
____ Your Turn Now Exercises: 1–7, SE pages 220–221
____ Concept Check: TE page 221
____ Getting Ready to Practice Exercises: 1–11, SE page 221

Chapter Pacing Guide	
Day	**Lesson**
1	**5.1;** 5.2
2	5.3; 5.4
3	5.5
4	5.6; 5.7 (begin)
5	5.7 (end); 5.8
6	Ch. 5 Review and Projects

APPLY/HOMEWORK

Homework Assignment

____ Block Schedule: pp. 222–223 Exs. 16–30, 34–44, 49–64 (with 5.2)

Reteaching the Lesson

____ Practice: CRB pages 7–9 (Level A, Level B, Level C); Practice Workbook
____ Study Guide: CRB pages 10–11; Spanish Study Guide

Extending the Lesson

____ Challenge: SE page 223; CRB page 12

ASSESSMENT OPTIONS

____ Daily Quiz (5.1): TE page 223 or Transparencies
____ Test-Taking Practice: SE page 223

Notes ____________

____

____

Name ______________________________ Date __________

Practice A

For use with pages 219–223

1. Write the fraction that has a denominator of 7 and a numerator of 3.
2. What addition problem does the model represent?

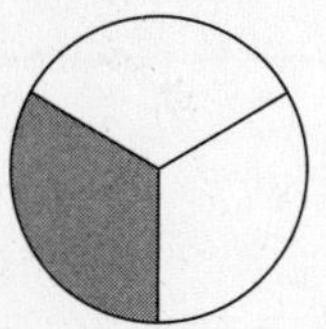 + 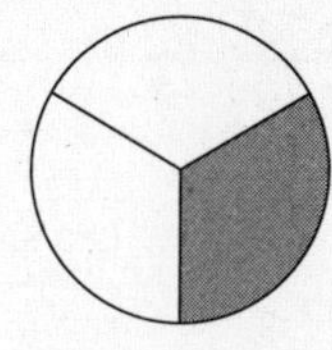 = 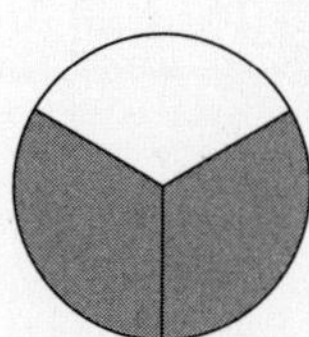

Find the sum or difference. Then simplify if possible.

3. $\frac{5}{9} + \frac{1}{9}$
4. $\frac{12}{17} - \frac{8}{17}$
5. $\frac{2}{5} - \frac{4}{5}$
6. $2\frac{1}{4} + \frac{3}{4}$
7. $\frac{19}{21} + \frac{13}{21}$
8. $4\frac{2}{7} - 1\frac{5}{7}$
9. $-2\frac{4}{5} + \frac{3}{5}$
10. $-9\frac{11}{15} - \frac{7}{15}$
11. $-6\frac{8}{11} - 6\frac{8}{11}$

In Exercises 12–17, simplify the expression.

12. $\frac{d}{12} + \frac{7d}{12}$
13. $\frac{9x}{10} - \frac{3x}{10}$
14. $\frac{13g}{24} - \frac{9g}{24}$
15. $-\frac{4m}{11} - \frac{7m}{11}$
16. $\frac{12w}{13} + \frac{5w}{13}$
17. $-\frac{3p}{12} + \frac{9p}{12}$
18. Today you ran $3\frac{1}{8}$ miles for track practice. Yesterday you ran $2\frac{5}{8}$ miles for practice. How much farther did you run at today's practice than at yesterday's practice?
19. Stacy was making a loaf of bread and the recipe called for $4\frac{1}{3}$ cups of flour. She decided to add an additional $\frac{2}{3}$ cup of flour. How much flour did she use altogether?

Evaluate.

20. $\frac{7}{15} + \frac{4}{15} + \frac{3}{15}$
21. $-\frac{4}{9} - \frac{7}{9} - \frac{1}{9}$
22. $\frac{5}{8} - 1\frac{3}{8} + \frac{7}{8}$
23. $-\frac{4}{21} + 2\frac{1}{21} - \frac{8}{21}$
24. $-4\frac{8}{17} - 2\frac{4}{17} + \frac{9}{17}$
25. $\frac{9}{10} - 2\frac{3}{10} + 1\frac{7}{10}$

Name ______________________ Date ________

Practice B

For use with pages 219–223

1. What subtraction problem does the model represent?

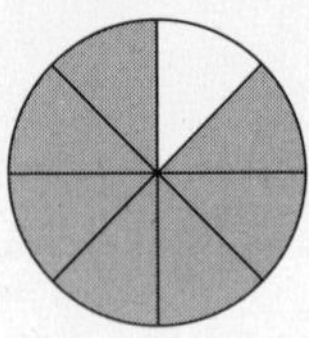 − 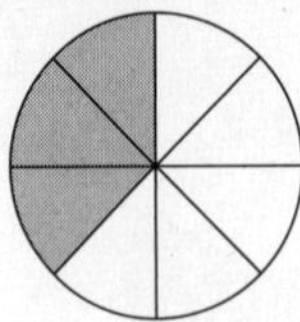 = 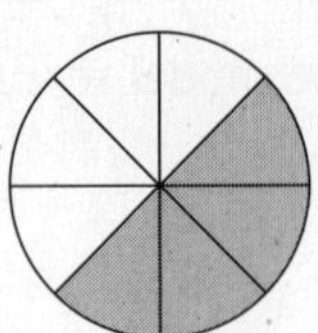

Lesson 5.1

Find the sum or difference.

2. $\frac{15}{24} + \frac{6}{24}$ **3.** $\frac{4}{9} - \frac{7}{9}$ **4.** $\frac{11}{12} - \frac{5}{12}$

5. $2\frac{3}{4} + \frac{3}{4}$ **6.** $-3\frac{4}{5} + 1\frac{2}{5}$ **7.** $\frac{8}{21} + \frac{6}{21}$

8. $-\frac{5}{6} - \left(-\frac{1}{6}\right)$ **9.** $-2\frac{1}{4} - 2\frac{1}{4}$ **10.** $4\frac{3}{8} + \left(-\frac{7}{8}\right)$

In Exercises 11–13, simplify the expression.

11. $\frac{5h}{6} + \frac{3h}{6}$ **12.** $\frac{3x}{5y} - \frac{4x}{5y}$ **13.** $-\frac{5v}{16w} - \frac{11v}{16w}$

14. A restaurant serves a steak that weighs $1\frac{5}{8}$ pounds. There is a bone in the steak that weighs $\frac{7}{8}$ of a pound. How much does the meat weigh?

15. Matthew worked $2\frac{1}{6}$ hours mowing lawns on Sunday. On Monday he mowed for $2\frac{5}{6}$ hours, and on Tuesday he mowed for $1\frac{5}{6}$ hours. What is the total amount of time Matthew spent mowing lawns in the 3 days?

Evaluate.

16. $\frac{9}{14} + \frac{3}{14} + \frac{1}{14}$ **17.** $-\frac{3}{22} - \frac{7}{22} - \frac{1}{22}$ **18.** $\frac{5}{9} - 1\frac{7}{9} + \frac{8}{9}$

19. $-\frac{13}{18} + 1\frac{5}{18} - \frac{17}{18}$ **20.** $-4\frac{9}{20} - 2\frac{13}{20} + \frac{7}{20}$ **21.** $3\frac{7}{12} - \left(1\frac{5}{12} - \frac{9}{12}\right)$

Solve the equation.

22. $x + \frac{1}{6} = \frac{5}{6}$ **23.** $\frac{13}{15} - w = \frac{7}{15}$ **24.** $b - \frac{3}{8} = \frac{7}{8}$

Name ____________________ Date __________

Practice C

For use with pages 219–223

Find the sum or difference.

1. $\frac{13}{15} + \frac{8}{15}$
2. $\frac{5}{14} - \frac{13}{14}$
3. $\frac{6}{7} - \frac{4}{7}$
4. $3\frac{3}{24} + \frac{13}{24}$
5. $-2\frac{3}{16} + 1\frac{15}{16}$
6. $3\frac{4}{21} + \left(-\frac{16}{21}\right)$
7. $-2\frac{5}{9} - 2\frac{5}{9}$
8. $-6\frac{12}{23} - \frac{17}{23}$
9. $-4\frac{4}{5} + \left(-2\frac{2}{5}\right)$

In Exercises 10–12, simplify the expression.

10. $\frac{5a}{12} + \frac{11a}{12}$
11. $-\frac{4m}{15n} + \frac{13m}{15n}$
12 $-\frac{5g}{24h} - \frac{17g}{24h}$

13. Cindy babysat for $5\frac{7}{10}$ hours on Friday night. She babysat for $4\frac{1}{10}$ hours on Sunday night. Cindy also babysat on Saturday night. She babysat a total of 17 hours over the weekend. How many hours did she babysit on Saturday?

14. David flew on a long distance airplane flight that took $20\frac{1}{4}$ hours. One section of the flight took $5\frac{3}{4}$ hours, and a second section took 10 hours. How long did the rest of the flight take?

Evaluate.

15. $\frac{8}{15} + \frac{4}{15} + \frac{11}{15}$
16. $-\frac{17}{30} - \frac{9}{30} - \frac{12}{30}$
17. $-\frac{13}{18} + \frac{5}{18} + \frac{11}{18}$
18. $\frac{23}{24} - 1\frac{17}{24} + \frac{9}{24}$
19. $-\frac{9}{10} + 2\frac{3}{10} - 1\frac{7}{10}$
20. $3\frac{9}{28} - 2\frac{13}{28} + \frac{5}{28}$
21. $\frac{-13}{19} + \frac{8}{19} - 1\frac{6}{19}$
22. $3\frac{17}{20} - \left(1\frac{9}{20} - \frac{13}{20}\right)$
23. $2\frac{7}{26} - 1\frac{15}{26} - \frac{21}{26}$

Solve the equation.

24. $a + \frac{2}{5} = \frac{4}{5}$
25. $\frac{23}{24} - p = \frac{9}{24}$
26. $m - \frac{8}{13} = \frac{7}{13}$

Find the value that makes the equation true.

27. $\frac{11}{12} + \frac{5}{12} - \underline{\quad} = \frac{9}{12}$
28. $\frac{5}{8} + \frac{3}{8} - \underline{\quad} = \frac{7}{8}$
29. $\underline{\quad} + \frac{4}{13} - \frac{7}{13} = \frac{9}{13}$

Name ______________________________ Date __________

Study Guide

For use with pages 219–223

GOAL **Add and subtract fractions with common denominators.**

VOCABULARY

Adding and Subtracting Fractions

To add fractions or subtract fractions with a common denominator, write the sum or difference of the numerators over the denominator. To add or subtract mixed numbers, find the sum or difference of the whole numbers and the sum or difference of the fractions. Then combine these quantities.

Lesson 5.1

EXAMPLE 1 Adding and Subtracting Fractions and Mixed Numbers

a. $4\frac{1}{6} + 7\frac{5}{6} = (4 + 7) + \left(\frac{1}{6} + \frac{5}{6}\right)$

$= 11 + \frac{6}{6}$

$= 11 + 1 = 12$

b. $5\frac{2}{7} - 2\frac{6}{7} = 4\frac{9}{7} - 2\frac{6}{7}$ $\quad \frac{2}{7} < \frac{6}{7}$, so rename $5\frac{2}{7}$ so that its fraction part is greater than $\frac{6}{7}$.

$= (4 - 2) + \left(\frac{9}{7} - \frac{6}{7}\right)$

$= 2 + \frac{3}{7} = 2\frac{3}{7}$

Exercises for Example 1

Find the sum or difference. Then simplify if possible.

1. $\frac{5}{11} + \frac{3}{11}$ **2.** $2\frac{3}{5} - 1\frac{2}{5}$ **3.** $4\frac{1}{7} - 2\frac{3}{7}$

EXAMPLE 2 Simplifying Fractions with Variables

$\frac{16y}{5} - \frac{y}{5} = \frac{16y - y}{5}$ Write difference over common denominator.

$= \frac{15y}{5}$ Combine like terms.

$= \frac{\overset{1}{\cancel{5}} \cdot 3 \cdot y}{\underset{1}{\cancel{5}}}$ Divide out common factor.

$= 3y$ Multiply.

Name ______________________________ Date __________

Study Guide

For use with pages 219–223

Exercises for Example 2

Find the sum or difference. Then simplify if possible.

4. $-\frac{a}{9} + \frac{2a}{9}$ **5.** $\frac{5}{8y} - \frac{2}{8y}$ **6.** $\frac{3x}{7} + \frac{3x}{7}$

EXAMPLE 3 Subtracting Mixed Numbers

Susan caught a fish that weighed $5\frac{3}{4}$ pounds. Emma caught a fish that weighed $7\frac{1}{4}$ pounds. How much heavier was Emma's fish?

$7\frac{1}{4} - 5\frac{3}{4} = 6\frac{5}{4} - 5\frac{3}{4}$ $\frac{1}{4} < \frac{3}{4}$, so rename $7\frac{1}{4}$ so that its fraction part is greater than $\frac{3}{4}$.

$= \left(6 + \frac{5}{4}\right) - \left(5 + \frac{3}{4}\right)$

$= 6 + \frac{5}{4} - 5 - \frac{3}{4}$ Remember to distribute the subtraction sign.

$= (6 - 5) + \left(\frac{5}{4} - \frac{3}{4}\right)$

$= 1 + \frac{2}{4} = 1\frac{1}{2}$

Answer: Emma's fish was $1\frac{1}{2}$ pounds heavier.

EXAMPLE 4 Evaluating with More than Two Terms

$5\frac{10}{11} - 3\frac{5}{11} + 4\frac{2}{11} = (5 - 3 + 4) + \left(\frac{10}{11} - \frac{5}{11} + \frac{2}{11}\right)$ Group whole numbers and fractions.

$= 6 + \frac{7}{11} = 6\frac{7}{11}$ Evaluate inside parentheses.

Exercises for Examples 3 and 4

7. A tailor cut a piece of material $4\frac{2}{3}$ inches long from a piece of material that was $10\frac{1}{3}$ inches long. How many inches of material are left?

Evaluate then simplify if possible.

8. $\frac{2}{9} + \frac{4}{9} - \frac{1}{9}$ **9.** $\frac{5}{12} - \frac{1}{12} + \frac{7}{12}$ **10.** $4\frac{1}{8} - 3\frac{3}{8} + 2\frac{5}{8}$

Name ______________________________ Date __________

Challenge Practice

For use with pages 219–223

In Exercises 1–6, solve the equation.

1. $\frac{x-1}{7} + \frac{2x}{7} = \frac{2}{7}$

2. $\frac{x-6}{3} - \frac{5}{3} = \frac{8}{3}$

3. $\frac{4}{x} + \frac{x+2}{x} = \frac{3}{x}$

4. $\frac{3}{x+2} + \frac{x-4}{x+2} = \frac{2x}{x+2}$

5. $\frac{2x+5}{x+3} + \frac{6x-4}{x+3} = \frac{17}{x+3}$

6. $\frac{x+2}{3x+1} - \frac{2x+2}{3x+1} = \frac{13}{3x+1}$

7. Describe and correct the error.

$$\frac{x-5}{x} - \frac{x+8}{x} = \frac{x-5-x+8}{x}$$
$$= \frac{3}{x}$$

Find the missing side length in the figure.

8. $P = 11\frac{7}{8}$ ft

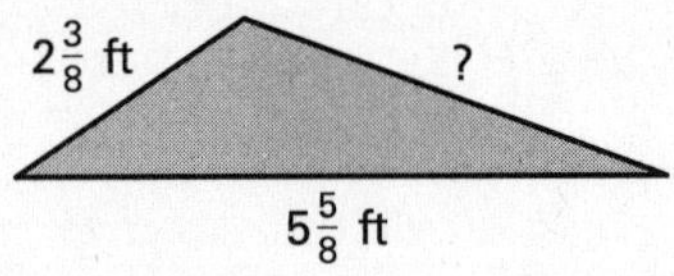

9. $P = 16$ m

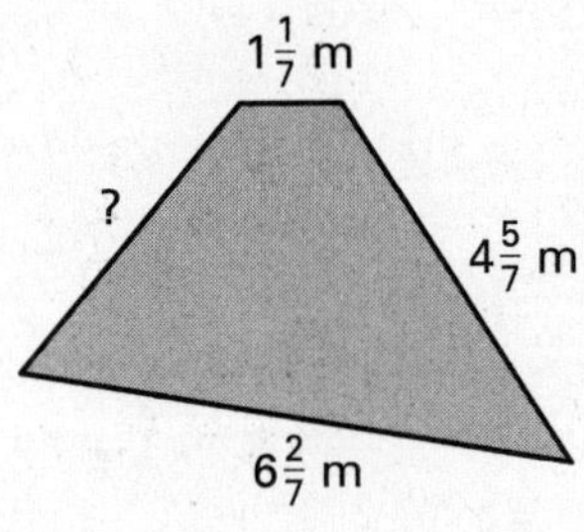

Teacher's Name ______________________ Class ______ Room ______ Date ______

Lesson Plan

1-day lesson (See *Pacing and Assignment Guide*, TE page 216A)

For use with pages 224–227

GOAL **Add and subtract fractions with different denominators.**

State/Local Objectives ______________________________________

____

✓ Check the items you wish to use for this lesson.

STARTING OPTIONS

____ Homework Check (5.1): TE page 222; Answer Transparencies
____ Homework Quiz (5.1): TE page 223; Transparencies
____ Warm-Up Transparencies

TEACHING OPTIONS

____ Notetaking Guide
____ Examples: 1–3, SE pages 224–225
____ Extra Examples: TE page 225
____ Your Turn Now Exercises: 1–8, SE pages 224–225
____ Concept Check: TE page 225
____ Getting Ready to Practice Exercises: 1–6, SE page 226

APPLY/HOMEWORK

Homework Assignment

____ Basic: pp. 226–227 Exs. 7–19, 21–28, 30, 34–42
____ Average: pp. 226–227 Exs. 9–20, 23–32, 34–43
____ Advanced: pp. 226–227 Exs. 11–20, 23–37*, 40–43

Reteaching the Lesson

____ Practice: CRB pages 15–17 (Level A, Level B, Level C); Practice Workbook
____ Study Guide: CRB pages 18–19; Spanish Study Guide

Extending the Lesson

____ Real-World Problem Solving: CRB page 20
____ Challenge: SE page 227; CRB page 21

ASSESSMENT OPTIONS

____ Daily Quiz (5.2): TE page 227 or Transparencies
____ Test-Taking Practice: SE page 227

Notes ______________________________________

____

____

Lesson 5.2

LESSON 5.2

Teacher's Name ______________________ Class ______ Room ______ Date ______

Lesson Plan for Block Scheduling

Half-block lesson (See *Pacing and Assignment Guide*, TE page 216A)

For use with pages 224–227

GOAL **Add and subtract fractions with different denominators.**

State/Local Objectives ____

____

✓ Check the items you wish to use for this lesson.

STARTING OPTIONS

____ Homework Check (5.1): TE page 222; Answer Transparencies
____ Homework Quiz (5.1): TE page 223; Transparencies
____ Warm-Up: Transparencies

TEACHING OPTIONS

____ Notetaking Guide
____ Examples: 1–3, SE pages 224–225
____ Extra Examples: TE page 225
____ Your Turn Now Exercises: 1–8, SE pages 224–225
____ Concept Check: TE page 225
____ Getting Ready to Practice Exercises: 1–6, SE page 226

Chapter Pacing Guide	
Day	**Lesson**
1	5.1; **5.2**
2	5.3; 5.4
3	5.5
4	5.6; 5.7 (begin)
5	5.7 (end); 5.8
6	Ch. 5 Review and Projects

APPLY/HOMEWORK

Homework Assignment

____ Block Schedule: pp. 226–227 Exs. 9–20, 23–32, 34–43 (with 5.1)

Reteaching the Lesson

____ Practice: CRB pages 15–17 (Level A, Level B, Level C); Practice Workbook
____ Study Guide: CRB pages 18–19; Spanish Study Guide

Extending the Lesson

____ Real-World Problem Solving: CRB page 20
____ Challenge: SE page 227; CRB page 21

ASSESSMENT OPTIONS

____ Daily Quiz (5.2): TE page 227 or Transparencies
____ Test-Taking Practice: SE page 227

Notes ____

____

____

LESSON 5.2

Name ______________________________ Date __________

Practice A

For use with pages 224–227

Find the least common denominator of the two fractions.

1. $\frac{1}{4}, \frac{3}{8}$
2. $\frac{2}{5}, \frac{5}{6}$
3. $\frac{6}{7}, \frac{1}{3}$
4. $\frac{7}{12}, \frac{9}{16}$

Match the expression with its solution.

5. $-\frac{14}{24} + \frac{1}{2}$
6. $1\frac{1}{2} + \frac{-5}{12}$
7. $\frac{1}{4} + \frac{1}{3}$
8. $\frac{11}{12} - \frac{5}{6}$

A. $\frac{7}{12}$

B. $1\frac{1}{12}$

C. $\frac{1}{12}$

D. $-\frac{1}{12}$

Find the sum or the difference.

9. $\frac{3}{4} - \frac{1}{2}$
10. $\frac{1}{6} + \frac{11}{12}$
11. $\frac{2}{3} + \frac{3}{4}$
12. $\frac{3}{8} - \frac{4}{5}$
13. $-\frac{7}{10} + \frac{11}{12}$
14. $\frac{5}{6} + \frac{-7}{8}$
15. $3\frac{1}{4} - \frac{7}{12}$
16. $5\frac{2}{7} - 6$
17. $4\frac{5}{8} + 3\frac{7}{15}$

In Exercises 18–20, use the following information. You volunteered to work 20 hours at your town's festival. You worked $7\frac{1}{8}$ hours the first day and $4\frac{5}{9}$ hours the second day. How many hours do you need to work the third day to complete your 20 hours?

18. Write a verbal model to describe the problem.
19. Substitute the given values and a variable for the unknown value into the model.
20. Solve the algebraic model to find the number of hours you need to volunteer on the third day.

Tell whether the statement is *true* or *false*.

21. $\frac{2}{3} + \frac{4}{5} - \frac{5}{6} = \frac{19}{30}$
22. $1\frac{3}{5} - \frac{8}{9} - \frac{11}{15} = -\frac{1}{45}$
23. $\frac{7}{16} - \frac{5}{8} + \frac{1}{4} = \frac{3}{16}$

Simplify the variable expression.

24. $\frac{4h}{3} - \frac{4h}{5}$
25. $\frac{10x}{3} - \frac{5x}{7}$
26. $\frac{1}{4y} + \frac{2}{3}$
27. $\frac{13}{16w} + \frac{19}{24w}$

LESSON 5.2

Name ______________________ Date __________

Practice B

For use with pages 224–227

Find the sum or the difference.

1. $\frac{7}{8} - \frac{1}{4}$

2. $\frac{5}{9} + \frac{3}{10}$

3. $\frac{10}{13} + \frac{12}{15}$

4. $-\frac{8}{11} + \frac{3}{8}$

5. $\frac{9}{14} + \frac{-13}{20}$

6. $5\frac{3}{5} - 7$

7. $4\frac{2}{7} - \frac{1}{6}$

8. $2\frac{1}{3} + 6\frac{19}{21}$

9. $\frac{12}{13} + 3\frac{7}{8}$

In Exercises 10–14, use the table that shows the results of a pie eating contest.

10. How many pies did Jim eat?

11. How many pies did Stephanie eat?

12. How many pies did Jamal eat?

13. Who won the pie eating contest?

14. If the people running the contest made 40 pies, how many pies did they have left over after the 3 contestants ate their pies?

	Pies Eaten		
	Apple	**Blueberry**	**Cherry**
Jim	$3\frac{3}{4}$	$2\frac{1}{8}$	$5\frac{2}{5}$
Jamal	$4\frac{3}{8}$	$3\frac{1}{2}$	$3\frac{2}{3}$
Stephanie	$2\frac{3}{5}$	$3\frac{5}{8}$	$5\frac{2}{3}$

Tell whether the statement is *true* or *false*.

15. $\frac{1}{5} + \frac{7}{10} - \frac{3}{20} = \frac{17}{20}$

16. $\frac{16}{27} - \frac{1}{3} + \frac{5}{54} = \frac{19}{54}$

17. $\frac{3}{15} - \frac{7}{12} + \frac{-7}{30} = \frac{-13}{30}$

Simplify the variable expression.

18. $\frac{8x}{15} - \frac{8x}{9}$

19. $\frac{4m}{5} - \frac{9m}{11}$

20. $\frac{10}{13p} + \frac{2}{7}$

21. $\frac{17}{24q} + \frac{16}{21q}$

In Exercises 22–24, solve the equation.

22. $4\frac{7}{8} + 1\frac{3}{5} - x = 3\frac{39}{40}$

23. $8\frac{3}{4} - 2\frac{1}{9} - y = 2\frac{29}{36}$

24. $w + 3\frac{5}{8} - 5\frac{1}{4} = 1\frac{3}{16}$

25. You need to dig a ditch $15\frac{1}{2}$ yards long. You dig $7\frac{3}{8}$ yards in the morning and another $3\frac{1}{4}$ yards after lunch. How much more of the ditch is left to dig?

Lesson 5.2

LESSON 5.2

Name ____________________ Date __________

Practice C

For use with pages 224–227

3-9

In Exercises 1–9, find the sum or the difference.

12 - 20

1. $\frac{9}{10} - \frac{4}{5}$

2. $\frac{5}{16} + \frac{11}{12}$

3. $\frac{18}{25} + \frac{13}{24}$

4. $-\frac{12}{21} + \frac{7}{12}$

5. $\frac{17}{36} + \frac{-14}{15}$

6. $\frac{9}{13} + 3\frac{1}{4}$

7. $6\frac{2}{23} - 7$

8. $5\frac{12}{13} - \frac{3}{8}$

9. $4\frac{6}{7} + 2\frac{8}{11}$

10. Brenda wanted to buy $5\frac{1}{12}$ yards of fabric for a dress and $2\frac{8}{9}$ yards of the same fabric for a jacket. The store only had 8 yards of fabric in stock. Was Brenda able to purchase enough fabric?

11. Three customers order meat from the deli. The first customer wants $3\frac{3}{4}$ pounds of steak. The second customer wants $2\frac{5}{16}$ pounds of steak, and the third customer wants $4\frac{3}{8}$ pounds of steak. The deli attendant has 10 pounds of steak in stock. Will he be able to fill the orders of all 3 customers?

Tell whether the statement is *true* or *false*.

12. $\frac{1}{6} + \frac{3}{4} - \frac{7}{12} = \frac{5}{12}$

13. $\frac{9}{14} - \frac{7}{21} + \frac{5}{6} = 1\frac{1}{7}$

14. $\frac{19}{22} - \frac{17}{20} + \frac{-1}{4} = -\frac{51}{220}$

Simplify the variable expression.

15. $\frac{6x}{19} - \frac{5x}{18}$

16. $\frac{12a}{23} + \frac{14}{31}$

17. $\frac{12}{35f} + \frac{17}{30f}$

In Exercises 18–20, solve the equation.

18. $c + 6\frac{8}{15} - 9\frac{1}{6} = \frac{1}{6}$

19. $7\frac{5}{6} - 3\frac{2}{9} - b = 2\frac{5}{9}$

20. $3\frac{5}{9} + 2\frac{1}{7} - a = 1\frac{31}{315}$

21. The gold medal winning jump in the long jump at the 2000 Sydney Summer Olympics was $8\frac{11}{20}$ meters. The world record, which was set in 1984, is $8\frac{79}{100}$ meters. How much longer is the world record than the distance jumped at the 2000 Summer Olympics?

Name ______________________ Date __________

Study Guide

For use with pages 224–227

GOAL Add and subtract fractions with different denominators.

VOCABULARY

Rewriting Fractions

To add or subtract fractions with different denominators, first rewrite the fractions so the denominators are the same.

EXAMPLE 1 Adding and Subtracting Fractions

a. $\frac{7}{8} - \frac{3}{4} = \frac{7}{8} - \frac{6}{8}$ Rewrite fractions using LCD of 8.

$= \frac{7-6}{8}$ Write difference over LCD.

$= \frac{1}{8}$ Evaluate numerator.

b. $\frac{2}{3} + \frac{-2}{5} = \frac{10}{15} + \frac{-6}{15}$ Rewrite fractions using LCD of 15.

$= \frac{10-6}{15}$ Write sum over LCD.

$= \frac{4}{15}$ Evaluate numerator.

EXAMPLE 2 Simplifying Variable Expressions

a. $\frac{3x}{7} - \frac{2x}{3} = \frac{9x}{21} - \frac{14x}{21}$ Rewrite fractions using LCD of 21.

$= \frac{9x - 14x}{21}$ Write difference over LCD.

$= -\frac{5x}{21}$ Combine like terms.

b. $\frac{6}{y} + \frac{3}{4} = \left(\frac{6}{y} \cdot \frac{4}{4}\right) + \left(\frac{3}{4} \cdot \frac{y}{y}\right)$ Multiply $\frac{6}{y}$ by $\frac{4}{4}$ and $\frac{3}{4}$ by $\frac{y}{y}$ for LCD of $4y$.

$= \frac{24}{4y} + \frac{3y}{4y}$ Multiply inside parentheses.

$= \frac{24 + 3y}{4y}$ Write sum over LCD.

Lesson 5.2

Name ______________________ Date __________

Study Guide

For use with pages 224–227

Exercises for Examples 1 and 2

Find the sum or difference. Then simplify if possible.

1. $\frac{5}{6} + \frac{7}{10}$ **2.** $\frac{1}{4} - \frac{6}{15}$ **3.** $-\frac{3c}{7} + \frac{c}{2}$ **4.** $\frac{x}{5y} - \frac{5x}{7y}$

EXAMPLE 3 Modeling with Mixed Numbers

A wire is $24\frac{1}{4}$ inches long. You cut off a piece $7\frac{2}{3}$ inches long for one job and $14\frac{5}{6}$ inches long for another job. Find the length of the remaining piece of wire.

Remaining length = Original length – (Length for job 1 + Length for job 2)

$= 24\frac{1}{4} - \left(7\frac{2}{3} + 14\frac{5}{6}\right)$ Write an algebraic model.

$= 24\frac{3}{12} - \left(7\frac{8}{12} + 14\frac{10}{12}\right)$ Rewrite fractions using LCD of 12.

$= 24\frac{3}{12} - 22\frac{6}{12}$ Add inside parentheses.

$= 23\frac{15}{12} - 22\frac{6}{12}$ Rename $24\frac{3}{12}$ as $23\frac{15}{12}$.

$= (23 - 22) + \left(\frac{15}{12} - \frac{6}{12}\right)$ Group whole numbers and fractions.

$= 1 + \frac{9}{12}$ Subtract whole numbers and fractions.

$= 1 + \frac{3}{4}$ Simplify.

$= 1\frac{3}{4}$ Add.

Answer: The remaining piece of wire is $1\frac{3}{4}$ inches long.

Exercise for Example 3

5. A recipe for punch calls for $1\frac{1}{2}$ quarts of orange juice, $1\frac{1}{4}$ quarts of ginger ale, and $\frac{3}{4}$ quart of cranberry juice. How many quarts will the recipe make?

Name ______________________________ Date __________

Real-World Problem Solving

For use with pages 224–227

Lesson 5.2

Public Speaking

Many types of careers involve public speaking. In some careers, people only have to give presentations occasionally. Other careers require people to give presentations all the time.

In Exercises 1–4, use the following information.

Ted just graduated from college and started a new job. His job requires him to give a presentation once a week. Ted prepares for this all week long. His presentation, along with a group of other presentations, must be completed in $1\frac{1}{4}$ hours. Although Ted doesn't have a set number of minutes to speak, his presentation is the most important one, and all the others get whatever time is left. He typically writes down his time in a table and all the other presenters fill in their presentation times. All the times need to add up to $1\frac{1}{4}$ hours.

Presentation	First Week	Second Week	Third Week
A	$\frac{1}{6}$	$\frac{3}{12}$	$\frac{3}{10}$
B	$\frac{3}{12}$		$\frac{1}{5}$
C	$\frac{1}{12}$	$\frac{1}{5}$	$\frac{1}{4}$
D	$\frac{1}{4}$	$\frac{1}{6}$	
E		$\frac{4}{30}$	$\frac{13}{60}$
Ted	$\frac{5}{12}$	$\frac{7}{20}$	$\frac{9}{20}$

1. The first week, presenter E is the last to sign up. How much time was left over for his presentation? Write your answer as a fraction in simplest form.
2. The second week, presenter B was the last to sign up. How much time was left for him to present?
3. The third week, presenter D went to sign up and noticed that they had gone over the $1\frac{1}{4}$ hour limit. How much over are they?
4. Because Ted's presentation is the most important, he doesn't have to shorten his presentation the third week, but everyone else does. Presenters A, B, C, and E all shorten their times by $\frac{1}{12}$ hour. Find the presentation times for presenters A, B, C, D, and E.

LESSON 5.2

Name ______________________________ Date __________

Challenge Practice

For use with pages 224–227

Find the sum or difference.

1. $\frac{7}{108} + \left(-\frac{55}{144}\right)$

2. $-\frac{125}{5488} - \frac{27}{9604}$

3. $\left(-\frac{3}{8} - \frac{2}{3}\right) - \left(-1\frac{1}{8} - 3\right)$

4. $\left(-\frac{3}{5} - 2\frac{1}{2}\right) + \left(-\frac{1}{8} - 1\right)$

In Exercises 5–7, use the figure at the right that shows a computer desk you want to buy from a catalog.

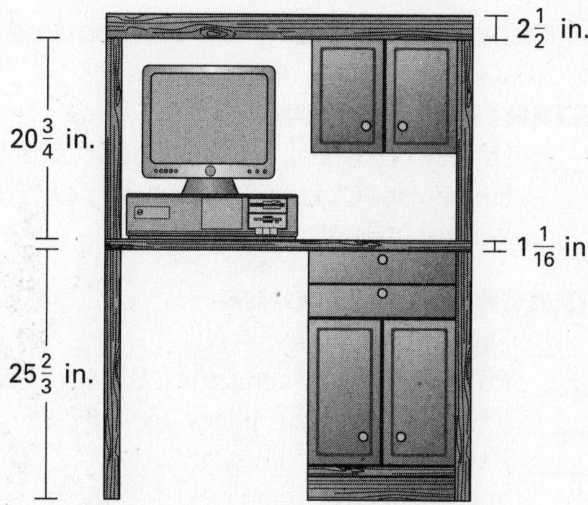

5. Find the total height of the computer desk.

6. Your computer monitor is $13\frac{5}{8}$ inches high, and your computer is $6\frac{7}{16}$ inches high. Will the monitor fit on top of the computer in the opening of the desk?

7. Use your answer to Exercise 6 and the figure at the right to find out how much space is needed or how much space remains.

In Exercises 8 and 9, use the circle graph at the right that shows the types of instruments in an orchestra.

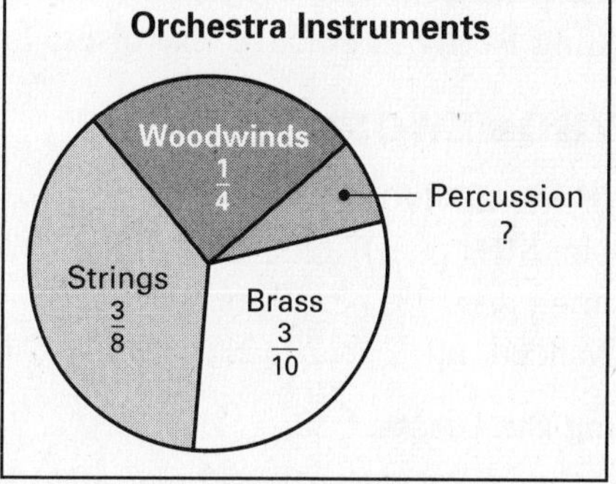

8. What fraction of the musicians play percussion instruments?

9. Find the difference between the greatest fraction of instruments and the least fraction of instruments. Write your answer in simplest form.

Lesson 5.2

LESSON 5.3

Teacher's Name ____________________ Class ______ Room ______ Date ______

Lesson Plan

1-day lesson (See *Pacing and Assignment Guide*, TE page 216A)

For use with pages 228–233

GOAL **Multiply fractions and mixed numbers.**

State/Local Objectives ____

____

✓ Check the items you wish to use for this lesson.

STARTING OPTIONS

____ Homework Check (5.2): TE page 226; Answer Transparencies
____ Homework Quiz (5.2): TE page 227; Transparencies
____ Warm-Up Transparencies

TEACHING OPTIONS

____ Notetaking Guide
____ Problem Solving Strategies: SE pages 228–229
____ Examples: 1–3, SE pages 230–231
____ Extra Examples: TE page 231
____ Your Turn Now Exercises: 1–8, SE page 231
____ Activity Master: CRB page 24
____ Concept Check: TE page 231
____ Getting Ready to Practice Exercises: 1–6, SE page 232

APPLY/HOMEWORK

Homework Assignment

____ Basic: SRH p. 707 Exs. 10–14; pp. 232–233 Exs. 7–18, 20–24, 26–29, 37–45
____ Average: pp. 232–233 Exs. 12–21, 24–34, 37–46
____ Advanced: pp. 232–233 Exs. 15–21, 24–36*, 39–46

Reteaching the Lesson

____ Practice: CRB pages 25–27 (Level A, Level B, Level C); Practice Workbook
____ Study Guide: CRB pages 28–29; Spanish Study Guide

Extending the Lesson

____ Challenge: SE page 233; CRB page 30

ASSESSMENT OPTIONS

____ Daily Quiz (5.3): TE page 233 or Transparencies
____ Test-Taking Practice: SE page 233

Notes ____

____

____

Teacher's Name ____________ Class ______ Room ______ Date ______

Lesson Plan for Block Scheduling

Half-block lesson (See *Pacing and Assignment Guide*, TE page 216A)

For use with pages 228–233

GOAL **Multiply fractions and mixed numbers.**

State/Local Objectives ____________

✓ **Check the items you wish to use for this lesson.**

Chapter Pacing Guide	
Day	**Lesson**
1	5.1; 5.2
2	**5.3;** 5.4
3	5.5
4	5.6; 5.7 (begin)
5	5.7 (end); 5.8
6	Ch. 5 Review and Projects

STARTING OPTIONS

____ Homework Check (5.2): TE page 226; Answer Transparencies
____ Homework Quiz (5.2): TE page 227; Transparencies
____ Warm-Up: Transparencies

TEACHING OPTIONS

____ Notetaking Guide
____ Problem Solving Strategies: SE pages 228–229
____ Examples: 1–3, SE pages 230–231
____ Extra Examples: TE page 231
____ Your Turn Now Exercises: 1–8, SE page 231
____ Activity Master: CRB page 24
____ Concept Check: TE page 231
____ Getting Ready to Practice Exercises: 1–6, SE page 232

APPLY/HOMEWORK

Homework Assignment

____ Block Schedule: pp. 232–233 Exs. 12–21, 24–34, 37–46 (with 5.4)

Reteaching the Lesson

____ Practice: CRB pages 25–27 (Level A, Level B, Level C); Practice Workbook
____ Study Guide: CRB pages 28–29; Spanish Study Guide

Extending the Lesson

____ Challenge: SE page 233; CRB page 30

ASSESSMENT OPTIONS

____ Daily Quiz (5.3): TE page 233 or Transparencies
____ Test-Taking Practice: SE page 233

Notes ____________

LESSON 5.3

Name ______________________________ Date ________

Activity Master

For use before Lesson 5.3

GOAL

Use a model to multiply fractions.

MATERIALS

- pencil
- graph paper

Exploring Fraction Multiplication

In this activity, you will use a model to multiply two fractions.

EXPLORE **Use graph paper to find the product $\frac{2}{3} \cdot \frac{3}{4}$.**

1. The denominators of the fractions are 3 and 4. Draw a 3 by 4 rectangle on graph paper.

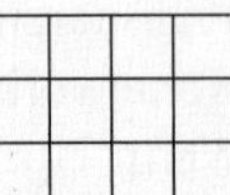

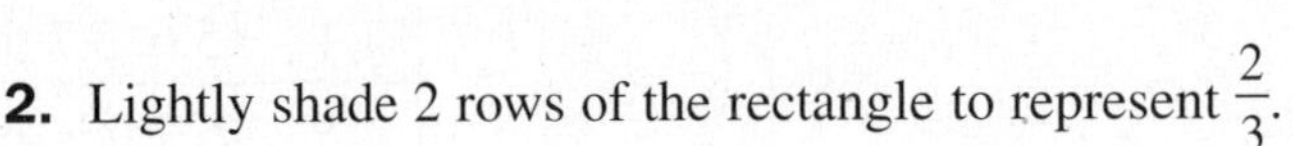

2. Lightly shade 2 rows of the rectangle to represent $\frac{2}{3}$.

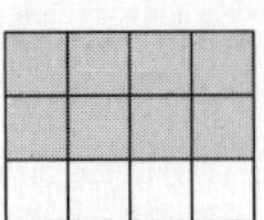

3. Shade 3 columns of the rectangle to represent $\frac{3}{4}$.

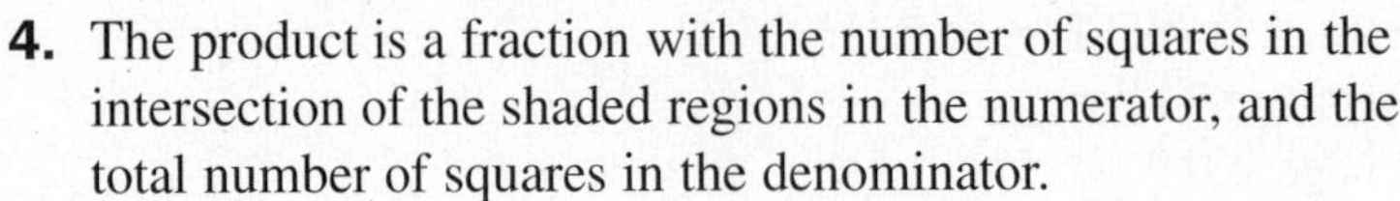

4. The product is a fraction with the number of squares in the intersection of the shaded regions in the numerator, and the total number of squares in the denominator.

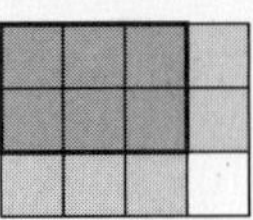

Answer: $\frac{2}{3} \cdot \frac{3}{4} = \frac{6}{12}$

Your Turn Now **Use graph paper to find the product. Do not simplify your answer.**

1. $\frac{3}{5} \cdot \frac{1}{4}$

2. $\frac{3}{5} \cdot \frac{5}{6}$

3. $\frac{1}{2} \cdot \frac{3}{7}$

4. $\frac{2}{9} \cdot \frac{2}{3}$

5. In Exercises 1–4, look for a pattern between the numerators of the fractions and the numerator of the product, and look for a pattern between the denominator of the fractions and the denominator of the product. Make a conjecture about the product of two fractions.

Name ______________________________ Date __________

Practice A

For use with pages 228–233

1. Complete the equation. $\frac{a}{b} \cdot \frac{c}{d} = \frac{a \cdot \_\_}{\_\_ \cdot d}$

2. To multiply mixed numbers, first write them as ____________________.

Match the expression with its solution.

3. $\frac{8}{15} \cdot \left(-3\frac{1}{4}\right)$ **4.** $-3 \cdot \frac{7}{45}$ **5.** $\frac{4}{5} \cdot \frac{2}{3}$ **6.** $2\frac{1}{3} \cdot 1\frac{1}{5}$

A. $-\frac{7}{15}$ **B.** $2\frac{4}{5}$ **C.** $-1\frac{11}{15}$ **D.** $\frac{8}{15}$

Find the product.

7. $\frac{4}{5} \cdot \frac{3}{7}$ **8.** $\frac{6}{13} \cdot \frac{5}{8}$ **9.** $\frac{9}{11} \cdot \frac{7}{18}$

10. $-8 \cdot \frac{1}{8}$ **11.** $15 \cdot \frac{14}{25}$ **12.** $-12 \cdot \left(-\frac{5}{6}\right)$

13. $3\frac{1}{8} \cdot 2\frac{7}{10}$ **14.** $-6\frac{3}{4} \cdot 4\frac{4}{9}$ **15.** $-7 \cdot \left(-1\frac{3}{8}\right)$

In Exercises 16–19, evaluate the expression when $a = \frac{3}{7}$ and $b = -\frac{8}{9}$.

16. $\frac{2}{3}a$ **17.** $-\frac{1}{5}b$ **18.** $1\frac{4}{7}b$ **19.** $7a$

20. The recipe for making 20 pancakes calls for $1\frac{1}{2}$ cups of milk. You need to make 120 pancakes for your pancake breakfast fundraiser. How many cups of milk will you need?

Find the area of the figure.

21.

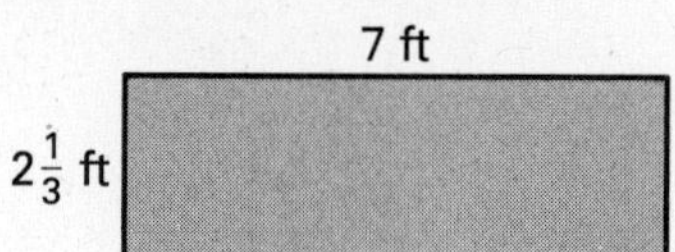

22.

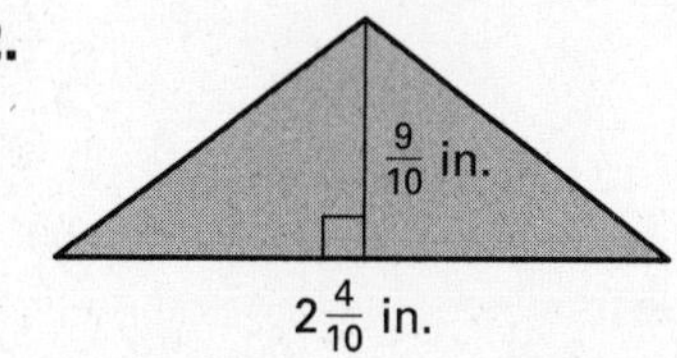

Name ______________________ Date __________

Practice B

For use with pages 228–233

Find the product.

1. $\frac{3}{10} \cdot \frac{1}{6}$
2. $\frac{7}{21} \cdot \frac{8}{9}$
3. $\frac{21}{25} \cdot \frac{15}{28}$
4. $-9 \cdot \frac{1}{9}$
5. $16 \cdot \frac{3}{4}$
6. $-18 \cdot \left(-\frac{7}{12}\right)$
7. $6\frac{4}{9} \cdot 4\frac{7}{10}$
8. $-7\frac{3}{5} \cdot 3\frac{4}{7}$
9. $-12 \cdot \left(-2\frac{7}{15}\right)$

Evaluate the expression when $x = \frac{7}{10}$ and $y = -\frac{11}{12}$.

10. $\frac{5}{9}x$
11. $-\frac{9}{13}y$
12. xy
13. $-2\frac{5}{8}y$

In Exercises 14 and 15, use the following information. Ice hockey is played on a rink that is 61 meters long and $25\frac{1}{2}$ meters wide. There are two goals on the hockey rink. Each goal opening has the shape of a rectangle that is $1\frac{1}{5}$ meters high and $1\frac{4}{5}$ meters wide.

14. What is the area of the ice hockey rink?
15. What is the area of a goal opening?

Find the area of the figure.

16.

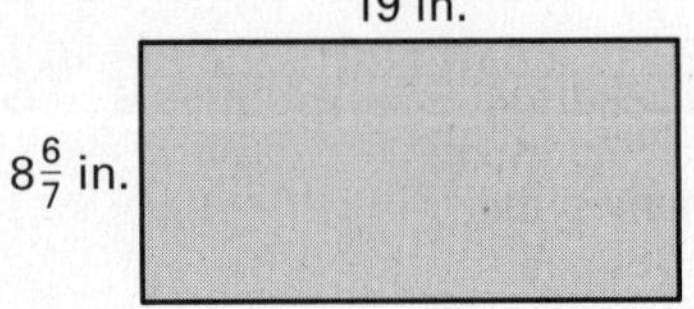

17.

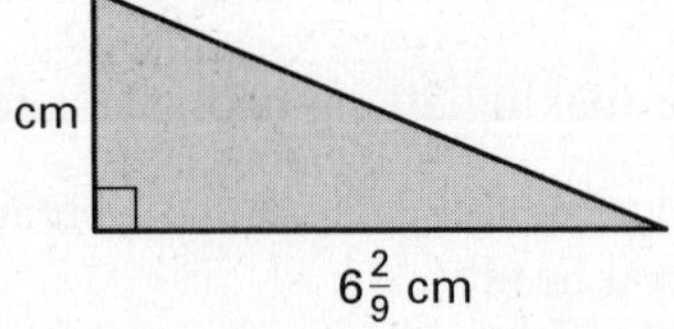

In Exercises 18–20, find the product.

18. $\frac{1}{3} \cdot \frac{2}{5} \cdot \left(-\frac{7}{9}\right)$
19. $-\frac{6}{7} \cdot 1\frac{2}{3} \cdot 4\frac{1}{5}$
20. $-7\frac{3}{5} \cdot \left(-1\frac{4}{7}\right) \cdot \frac{5}{8}$

21. Evaluate the expression $\frac{1}{9} + \frac{2}{5} \cdot \frac{11}{15}$.

Lesson 5.3

LESSON **5.3**

Name ______________________________ Date __________

Practice C

For use with pages 228–233

Find the product.

1. $\frac{7}{8} \cdot \frac{9}{14}$

2. $\frac{12}{21} \cdot \frac{35}{48}$

3. $\frac{24}{25} \cdot \frac{35}{36}$

4. $-12 \cdot \frac{1}{12}$

5. $15 \cdot \frac{13}{20}$

6. $-21 \cdot \left(-\frac{5}{9}\right)$

7. $7\frac{11}{12} \cdot 3\frac{8}{15}$

8. $-12\frac{4}{7} \cdot 4\frac{6}{11}$

9. $-24 \cdot \left(6\frac{5}{12}\right)$

In Exercises 10–13, evaluate the expression when $x = \frac{11}{15}$ and $y = -\frac{18}{25}$.

10. $\frac{3}{10}x$

11. $-\frac{7}{9}y$

12. xy

13. $-2\frac{8}{13}x$

14. The penalty area on a soccer field is $40\frac{8}{25}$ meters long and $16\frac{1}{2}$ meters wide. What is the area of the penalty area on a soccer field?

Find the area of the figure.

15.

$7\frac{4}{5}$ m

$2\frac{1}{9}$ m

16.

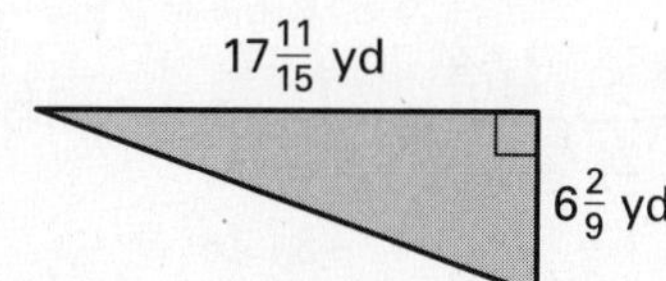

Find the product.

17. $\frac{1}{6} \cdot \frac{4}{9} \cdot \left(-\frac{11}{12}\right)$

18. $-\frac{12}{13} \cdot 2\frac{6}{7} \cdot 4\frac{3}{4}$

19. $-6\frac{19}{21} \cdot \left(-3\frac{8}{15}\right) \cdot \frac{5}{18}$

In Exercises 20–22, evaluate the expression.

20. $-\frac{7}{9} + 3\frac{1}{5} \cdot \frac{17}{20}$

21. $\frac{7}{4} \cdot \left(\frac{5}{12} - \frac{11}{30}\right)$

22. $7 - \left(\frac{1}{8} + \frac{1}{6}\right)^2$

23. A diamond's weight is measured in carats. A carat is equal to about $\frac{7}{1000}$ ounces. The largest diamond found had a weight of 3106 carats. This diamond was cut into 105 smaller diamonds. The largest piece has a weight of $530\frac{1}{5}$ carats. How many ounces does this piece weigh?

LESSON 5.3

Name ____________________ Date __________

Study Guide

For use with pages 228–233

GOAL **Multiply fractions and mixed numbers.**

VOCABULARY

Multiplying Fractions

The product of two or more fractions is equal to the product of the numerators divided by the product of the denominators.

EXAMPLE 1 Multiplying Fractions

a. $-\frac{2}{3} \cdot \left(-\frac{1}{6}\right) = \frac{-2 \cdot (-1)}{3 \cdot 6}$ Use rule for multiplying fractions.

$= \frac{2}{18}$ Evaluate numerator and denominator.

$= \frac{\not{2}^{1}}{\not{18}_{9}}$ Divide out common factors.

$= \frac{1}{9}$

b. $-\frac{5}{24} \cdot \frac{16}{25} = \frac{-5 \cdot 16}{24 \cdot 25}$ Use rule for multiplying fractions.

$= \frac{{}^{-1}\not{-5} \cdot \not{16}^{2}}{{}_{3}\not{24} \cdot \not{25}_{5}}$ Divide out common factors.

$= -\frac{2}{15}$ Multiply.

Exercises for Example 1

Find the product. Write your answer in simplest form.

1. $\frac{6}{15} \cdot 12$ **2.** $-\frac{2}{7} \cdot \frac{14}{9}$ **3.** $\frac{2}{3} \cdot \left(-\frac{3}{8}\right)$ **4.** $-\frac{2}{5} \cdot \left(-\frac{3}{4}\right)$

EXAMPLE 2 Multiplying Mixed Numbers

$1\frac{1}{3} \cdot \left(-2\frac{3}{7}\right) = \frac{4}{3} \cdot \left(-\frac{17}{7}\right)$ Write as improper fractions.

$= \frac{4 \cdot (-17)}{3 \cdot 7}$ Use rule for multiplying fractions.

$= -\frac{68}{21}$ Multiply.

$= -3\frac{5}{21}$ Write as a mixed number.

Lesson 5.3

LESSON 5.3 Continued

Name ______________________ Date __________

Study Guide

For use with pages 228–233

Exercises for Example 2

Find the product. Write your answer in simplest form.

5. $1\frac{1}{4} \cdot 2\frac{1}{8}$

6. $-3\frac{3}{8} \cdot 4\frac{2}{3}$

7. $1\frac{3}{4} \cdot 2\frac{2}{5}$

8. $-2\frac{3}{5} \cdot \left(-3\frac{5}{7}\right)$

EXAMPLE 3 Evaluating Variable Expressions

Evaluate $2x^3y$ when $x = -\frac{1}{2}$ and $y = -\frac{2}{5}$.

$2x^3y = 2\left(-\frac{1}{2}\right)^3 \cdot \left(-\frac{2}{5}\right)$ Substitute $-\frac{1}{2}$ for x and $-\frac{2}{5}$ for y.

$= \frac{2}{1} \cdot \left(-\frac{1}{2}\right) \cdot \left(-\frac{1}{2}\right) \cdot \left(-\frac{1}{2}\right) \cdot \left(-\frac{2}{5}\right)$ Write $-\frac{1}{2}$ as a factor 3 times.

$= \frac{2(-1)(-1)(-1)(-2)}{1(2)(2)(2)(5)}$ Use rule for multiplying fractions.

$= \frac{\overset{1}{\cancel{2}}(-1)(-1)(-1)(\overset{-1}{\cancel{-2}})}{1(\underset{1}{\cancel{2}})(\underset{1}{\cancel{2}})(2)(5)}$ Divide out common factors.

$= \frac{1}{10}$ Multiply.

Exercises for Example 3

Evaluate the expression when $x = -\frac{1}{6}$ and $y = \frac{4}{9}$.

9. $3xy$

10. $-\frac{1}{3}x$

11. xy^2

12. x^2y

Lesson 5.3

Name ______________________ Date __________

Challenge Practice

For use with pages 228-233

Find the product.

1. $\left(\frac{3}{4} - \frac{5}{6}\right)\left(\frac{2}{7} + \frac{3}{8}\right)$

2. $\left(\frac{3}{11} - \frac{5}{7}\right)\left(\frac{2}{3} + \frac{3}{4} - \frac{2}{5}\right)$

3. $7\frac{1}{12} \cdot 11\frac{2}{5} \cdot 8\frac{3}{8} \cdot 6\frac{1}{5}$

4. $\left(33\frac{1}{3} - 18\frac{1}{8}\right)\left(6\frac{3}{5} - 8\frac{3}{7}\right)$

5. In the previous lesson you learned that to find the sum of $9\frac{2}{7}$ and $3\frac{3}{4}$ you could add the whole numbers and fractions separately, and then find the total sum. Show that this method does not apply to finding the product of two mixed numbers.

6. Write an algebraic expression for the product of the given fraction and mixed number. $(b, e \neq 0)$

   $\frac{a}{b} \cdot c\frac{d}{e}$

Lesson 5.3

Teacher's Name ______________________ Class ______ Room ______ Date ______

Lesson Plan

1-day lesson (See *Pacing and Assignment Guide*, TE page 216A)

For use with pages 234–239

GOAL **Divide fractions.**

State/Local Objectives ____

____

✓ Check the items you wish to use for this lesson.

STARTING OPTIONS

____ Homework Check (5.3): TE page 232; Answer Transparencies
____ Homework Quiz (5.3): TE page 233; Transparencies
____ Warm-Up Transparencies

TEACHING OPTIONS

____ Notetaking Guide
____ Activity: SE page 234
____ Examples: 1–4, SE pages 234–236
____ Extra Examples: TE pages 235–236
____ Your Turn Now Exercises: 1–8, SE page 235
____ Keystrokes for Technology Activity 5.4 on SE page 239: CRB page 33
____ Concept Check: TE page 236
____ Getting Ready to Practice Exercises: 1–11, SE page 236

APPLY/HOMEWORK

Homework Assignment

____ Basic: EP p. 728 Exs. 21–24; pp. 237–238 Exs. 12–15, 20–23, 29–34, 36–39, 47–56
____ Average: pp. 237–238 Exs. 14–19, 24–28, 31–35, 38–43, 47–56
____ Advanced: pp. 237–238 Exs. 18–21, 28–36, 40–50*, 53–55

Reteaching the Lesson

____ Practice: CRB pages 34–36 (Level A, Level B, Level C); Practice Workbook
____ Study Guide: CRB pages 37–38; Spanish Study Guide

Extending the Lesson

____ Challenge: SE page 238; CRB page 39

ASSESSMENT OPTIONS

____ Daily Quiz (5.4): TE page 238 or Transparencies
____ Test-Taking Practice: SE page 238
____ Quiz (5.1–5.4): SE page 241; Assessment Book page 57

Notes ____

____

____

LESSON 5.4

Teacher's Name ______________________ Class ______ Room ______ Date ______

Lesson Plan for Block Scheduling

Half-block lesson (See *Pacing and Assignment Guide*, TE page 216A)

For use with pages 234–239

GOAL **Divide fractions.**

State/Local Objectives ____

____

✓ Check the items you wish to use for this lesson.

Chapter Pacing Guide	
Day	**Lesson**
1	5.1; 5.2
2	5.3; **5.4**
3	5.5
4	5.6; 5.7 (begin)
5	5.7 (end); 5.8
6	Ch. 5 Review and Projects

STARTING OPTIONS

____ Homework Check (5.3): TE page 232; Answer Transparencies
____ Homework Quiz (5.3): TE page 233; Transparencies
____ Warm-Up: Transparencies

TEACHING OPTIONS

____ Notetaking Guide
____ Activity: SE page 234
____ Examples: 1–4, SE pages 234–236
____ Extra Examples: TE pages 235–236
____ Your Turn Now Exercises: 1–8, SE page 235
____ Keystrokes for Technology Activity 5.4 on SE page 239: CRB page 33
____ Concept Check: TE page 236
____ Getting Ready to Practice Exercises: 1–11, SE page 236

APPLY/HOMEWORK

Homework Assignment

____ Block Schedule: pp. 237–238 Exs. 14–19, 24–28, 31–35, 38–43, 47–56 (with 5.3)

Reteaching the Lesson

____ Practice: CRB pages 34–36 (Level A, Level B, Level C); Practice Workbook
____ Study Guide: CRB pages 37–38; Spanish Study Guide

Extending the Lesson

____ Challenge: SE page 238; CRB page 39

ASSESSMENT OPTIONS

____ Daily Quiz (5.4): TE page 238 or Transparencies
____ Test-Taking Practice: SE page 238
____ Quiz (5.1–5.4): SE page 241; Assessment Book page 57

Notes ____

____

____

Name ______________________ Date ________

Technology Activity Keystrokes

For use with Technology Activity 5.4, page 239

TI-34 II

To set the calculator to display mixed numbers, press 2nd **[FracMode],** cursor to A⌴b/c, and press ENTER. To set the calculator to display fractions in simplest form, press 2nd **[FracMode],** cursor to Auto, and press ENTER.

a. 2 / 3 − 4 UNIT 6 / 7 ENTER

b. (-) 5 / 17 × (-) 8 / 35 ENTER

c. 3 / 10 ÷ (-) 1 UNIT 4 / 5 ENTER

TI-73

To set the calculator to display mixed numbers, press MODE, cursor to A⌴b/c, and press ENTER. To set the calculator to display fractions in simplest form, press MODE, cursor to Autosimp, and press ENTER.

a. 2 b/c 3 ▶ − 4 UNIT 6 ▼ 7 ENTER

b. (-) 5 b/c 17 ▶ × (-) 8 b/c 35 ENTER

c. 3 b/c 10 ▶ ÷ (-) 1 UNIT 4 ▼ 5 ENTER

LESSON 5.4

Name ______________________________ Date __________

Practice A

For use with pages 234–239

1. What division problem does the model represent? What is the solution?

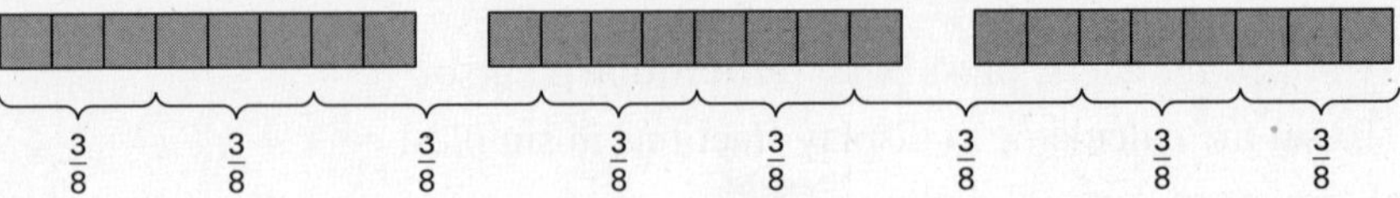

Write the reciprocal of the number.

2. $\frac{7}{9}$ **3.** $-\frac{1}{11}$ **4.** 6 **5.** $-2\frac{4}{5}$

Find the quotient.

6. $\frac{5}{6} \div \frac{1}{12}$ **7.** $-\frac{5}{7} \div \frac{2}{9}$ **8.** $\frac{10}{17} \div \left(-\frac{7}{8}\right)$

9. $\frac{21}{25} \div \left(-\frac{5}{11}\right)$ **10.** $\frac{1}{3} \div 6$ **11.** $\frac{7}{9} \div (-14)$

12. $8\frac{4}{9} \div 3\frac{1}{6}$ **13.** $6\frac{7}{12} \div \left(-2\frac{1}{4}\right)$ **14.** $-4\frac{5}{6} \div 3\frac{7}{8}$

15. $9\frac{1}{4} \div 7$ **16.** $3\frac{11}{15} \div (-4)$ **17.** $4\frac{20}{21} \div 2\frac{2}{3}$

Solve the equation.

18. $\frac{1}{9}x = 3$ **19.** $-\frac{2}{5}y = -4$ **20.** $22 = -\frac{11}{12}w$

In Exercises 21–23, use the following information. A catering company has 12 pies to serve to the guests at a dinner party. Each guest is served $\frac{1}{8}$ of a pie. How many guests will they be able to serve?

21. Write a verbal model.

22. Substitute the given values into the model.

23. Solve the equation.

24. A box of cereal contains $25\frac{1}{2}$ ounces of cereal. The recommended serving size is $2\frac{1}{10}$ ounces. How many servings are there in the box?

Lesson 5.4

Name ______________________ Date __________

Practice B

For use with pages 234–239

Write the reciprocal of the number.

1. $\frac{3}{17}$ **2.** $-\frac{7}{22}$ **3.** 12 **4.** $3\frac{9}{10}$

Find the quotient.

5. $\frac{1}{4} \div \frac{7}{8}$ **6.** $-\frac{2}{9} \div \frac{5}{6}$ **7.** $\frac{7}{15} \div \frac{11}{14}$

8. $\frac{17}{24} \div \left(-\frac{8}{13}\right)$ **9.** $\frac{15}{26} \div 5$ **10.** $\frac{18}{33} \div (-12)$

11. $4\frac{1}{8} \div 2\frac{2}{5}$ **12.** $7\frac{5}{6} \div \left(-9\frac{4}{7}\right)$ **13.** $-6\frac{13}{32} \div \left(-3\frac{3}{16}\right)$

14. $2\frac{17}{20} \div (-4)$ **15.** $3\frac{9}{14} \div 7$ **16.** $-9\frac{4}{21} \div 1\frac{8}{9}$

In Exercises 17–19, solve the equation.

17. $\frac{7}{8}a = 14$ **18.** $-\frac{9}{10}b = 27$ **19.** $-14 = -\frac{2}{13}w$

20. You mix a quart of grape juice in a pitcher. You are filling juice glasses that each hold $\frac{2}{3}$ cup of juice. There are 4 cups in a quart. How many juice glasses can you fill?

21. A child is playing with blocks and wants to build a house with a roof. The pieces to build the roof are $\frac{3}{4}$ inch wide. The entire roof will be $7\frac{5}{8}$ inches wide. How many pieces laid side-by-side will cover the width?

In Exercises 22–24, evaluate the expression when $x = 3$ and $y = 7$.

22. $\frac{x}{4} \div \frac{9}{120}$ **23.** $\frac{2}{9}x \div \frac{4y}{15}$ **24.** $-\frac{20}{y} \div \frac{x}{21}$

25. A team is playing soccer on a field that is $110\frac{2}{5}$ yards long. The field has an area of $10{,}852\frac{8}{25}$ square yards. How wide is the field?

Lesson 5.4

Name ______________________________ Date __________

Practice C

For use with pages 234–239

1. Are the numbers $\frac{1}{17}$ and -17 reciprocals? Explain.

Find the quotient.

2. $\frac{5}{9} \div \frac{3}{8}$

3. $\frac{11}{12} \div \left(-\frac{8}{11}\right)$

4. $-\frac{13}{20} \div \frac{15}{24}$

5. $\frac{14}{27} \div \left(-\frac{7}{15}\right)$

6. $\frac{8}{35} \div 16$

7. $\frac{10}{11} \div (-22)$

8. $6\frac{6}{7} \div 2\frac{1}{4}$

9. $4\frac{1}{5} \div \left(-8\frac{2}{3}\right)$

10. $-10\frac{5}{21} \div \left(-3\frac{4}{7}\right)$

11. $5\frac{7}{9} \div (-12)$

12. $6\frac{15}{22} \div 21$

13. $-9\frac{13}{27} \div 2\frac{1}{3}$

In Exercises 14–16, solve the equation.

14. $\frac{4}{13}g = 24$

15. $-\frac{24}{25}h = 8$

16. $-34 = -\frac{17}{20}j$

17. You are helping to cover a roof with asphalt shingles. The roof is $30\frac{1}{2}$ feet long. Each shingle is $3\frac{7}{25}$ feet long. How many shingles laid end-to-end in a row does it take to cover the length of the roof?

18. Toothpaste commercials claim 3 out of 4 dentists recommend a certain brand of toothpaste. If 273 dentists recommended this toothpaste, how many dentists were questioned? Explain how you got your answer.

In Exercises 19–21, evaluate the expression when $m = 5$ and $n = 12$.

19. $\frac{m}{24} \div \frac{25}{240}$

20. $\frac{3}{10}m \div \frac{n}{8}$

21. $-\frac{27}{n} \div \frac{m}{13}$

22. A checkerboard is 12 inches wide and 12 inches long. Each square on the board is $1\frac{1}{2}$ inches by $1\frac{1}{2}$ inches. If you did not know how many squares were on the board, how would you determine this from the given measurements? How many squares are there on the board?

LESSON 5.4

Name ______________________ Date __________

Study Guide

For use with pages 234–239

GOAL Divide fractions.

VOCABULARY

Two nonzero numbers are **reciprocals** if their product is 1. Reciprocals are also called **multiplicative inverses**.

Dividing Fractions

To divide by a fraction, multiply by its reciprocal.

$\frac{a}{b} \div \frac{c}{d} = \frac{a}{b} \cdot \frac{d}{c}$ $(b, c, d \neq 0)$

EXAMPLE 1 Dividing a Fraction by a Fraction

a. $\frac{14}{9} \div \frac{7}{18} = \frac{14}{9} \cdot \frac{18}{7}$

$= \frac{{}^{2}\cancel{14} \cdot \cancel{18}^{2}}{{}_{1}\cancel{9} \cdot \cancel{7}_{1}}$

$= 4$

b. $-\frac{3}{7} \div \frac{12}{21} = -\frac{3}{7} \cdot \frac{21}{12}$

$= \frac{{}^{-1}\cancel{-3} \cdot \cancel{21}^{3}}{{}_{1}\cancel{7} \cdot \cancel{12}_{4}}$

$= -\frac{3}{4}$

Exercises for Example 1

Find the quotient.

1. $\frac{2}{3} \div \frac{3}{5}$

2. $-\frac{11}{12} \div \frac{7}{8}$

3. $\frac{10}{13} \div \frac{15}{26}$

4. $-\frac{5}{6} \div \left(-\frac{4}{9}\right)$

EXAMPLE 2 Dividing a Fraction by a Whole Number

$\frac{9}{11} \div 18 = \frac{9}{11} \cdot \frac{1}{18}$ $18 \cdot \frac{1}{18} = 1$, so the reciprocal of $\frac{18}{1}$ is $\frac{1}{18}$.

$= \frac{{}^{1}\cancel{9} \cdot 1}{11 \cdot \cancel{18}_{2}}$ Use rule for multiplying fractions. Then divide out common factor.

$= \frac{1}{22}$ Simplify.

Exercises for Example 2

Find the quotient.

5. $-\frac{1}{6} \div 6$

6. $\frac{2}{7} \div 8$

7. $-\frac{3}{10} \div 12$

8. $-\frac{5}{14} \div 20$

Lesson 5.4

Name ________________________________ Date __________

Study Guide

For use with pages 234–239

EXAMPLE 3 Dividing Mixed Numbers

$1\frac{3}{5} \div \left(-2\frac{1}{2}\right) = \frac{8}{5} \div \left(-\frac{5}{2}\right)$ Write $1\frac{3}{5}$ and $-2\frac{1}{2}$ as improper fractions.

$= \frac{8}{5} \cdot \left(-\frac{2}{5}\right)$ Multiply by $-\frac{2}{5}$, the reciprocal of $-\frac{5}{2}$.

$= \frac{8 \cdot (-2)}{5 \cdot 5}$ Multiply fractions.

$= -\frac{16}{25}$ Multiply.

Exercises for Example 3

Find the quotient.

9. $12\frac{2}{3} \div \frac{4}{3}$

10. $1\frac{3}{8} \div 2\frac{1}{16}$

11. $-1\frac{7}{11} \div \frac{9}{11}$

12. $-3\frac{2}{3} \div \left(-2\frac{4}{9}\right)$

EXAMPLE 4 Solving an Equation with a Fraction

A carpenter is building a bookshelf to hold a set of books that are each $1\frac{5}{8}$ inches wide. How many books will fit on a shelf that is 26 inches long?

Length of bookshelf = width of each book • number of books

$26 = 1\frac{5}{8} \cdot n$ Write an algebraic model.

$26 = \frac{13}{8}n$ Write $1\frac{5}{8}$ as an improper fraction.

$\frac{8}{13} \cdot 26 = \frac{8}{13} \cdot \frac{13}{8} \cdot n$ Multiply each side by $\frac{8}{13}$, the reciprocal of $\frac{13}{8}$.

$\frac{8}{\cancel{13}_1} \cdot \frac{\cancel{26}^2}{1} = n$ Divide out common factor.

$16 = n$ Simplify.

Answer: 16 books will fit on the shelf.

Exercise for Example 4

13. Your cat eats about $\frac{3}{8}$ of a pound of cat food per day. How long should a 15 pound bag of cat food last?

Lesson 5.4

Name ______________________________ Date ____________

Challenge Practice

For use with pages 234 - 239

1. Name the only integer that does not have a reciprocal. Explain.

2. Name a positive number that is greater than its reciprocal.

3. Name a positive number that is less than its reciprocal.

4. Name a negative number that is greater than its reciprocal.

5. Name a negative number that is less than its reciprocal.

6. Name two numbers that are equal to their reciprocals.

In Exercises 7–10, find the quotient. Then simplify the expression.

7. $\frac{a^2 b}{c} \div \frac{ab}{c^2}$

8. $\frac{4x^2}{5y} \div \frac{y^2}{10x}$

9. $\frac{16x}{9y^2} \div \frac{x^3}{15y^4}$

10. $\frac{15ac^2}{7bd} \div \frac{4a}{14b^2 d}$

Lesson 5.4

LESSON 5.5

Teacher's Name ____________________________ Class ______ Room _______ Date_______

Lesson Plan

2-day lesson (See *Pacing and Assignment Guide*, TE page 216A)

For use with pages 242–246

GOAL **Write fractions as decimals and decimals as fractions.**

State/Local Objectives ____

____

✓ Check the items you wish to use for this lesson.

STARTING OPTIONS

____ Homework Check (5.4): TE page 237; Answer Transparencies
____ Homework Quiz (5.4): TE page 238; Transparencies
____ Warm-Up Transparencies

TEACHING OPTIONS

____ Notetaking Guide
____ Examples: Day 1: 1–2, SE pages 242–243; Day 2: 3–4, SE pages 243–244
____ Extra Examples: TE pages 243–244
____ Your Turn Now Exercises: Day 1: 1–2, SE page 243; Day 2: 3–10, SE page 244
____ Concept Check: TE page 244
____ Getting Ready to Practice Exercises: Day 1: 1–8, 13, SE page 244;
Day 2: 9–12, SE page 244

APPLY/HOMEWORK

Homework Assignment

____ Basic: Day 1: pp. 245–246 Exs. 14–21, 42–44, 53–59
Day 2: pp. 245–246 Exs. 26–37, 46–48, 60–62
____ Average: Day 1: pp. 245–246 Exs. 16–25, 42–46, 52–57
Day 2: pp. 245–246 Exs. 28–41, 47–50, 60–62
____ Advanced: Day 1: pp. 245–246 Exs. 18–25, 43–50, 60–62
Day 2: pp. 245–246 Exs. 30–41, 51–56*

Reteaching the Lesson

____ Practice: CRB pages 42–44 (Level A, Level B, Level C); Practice Workbook
____ Study Guide: CRB pages 45–46; Spanish Study Guide

Extending the Lesson

____ Challenge: SE page 246; CRB page 47

ASSESSMENT OPTIONS

____ Daily Quiz (5.5): TE page 246 or Transparencies
____ Test-Taking Practice: SE page 246

Notes ____

____

____

Teacher's Name ______________________ Class ______ Room _______ Date _______

Lesson Plan for Block Scheduling

1-block lesson (See *Pacing and Assignment Guide*, TE page 216A)
For use with pages 242–246

GOAL **Write fractions as decimals and decimals as fractions.**

State/Local Objectives ____

____

✓ Check the items you wish to use for this lesson.

Chapter Pacing Guide	
Day	**Lesson**
1	5.1; 5.2
2	5.3; 5.4
3	**5.5**
4	5.6; 5.7 (begin)
5	5.7 (end); 5.8
6	Ch. 5 Review and Projects

STARTING OPTIONS

____ Homework Check (5.4): TE page 237; Answer Transparencies
____ Homework Quiz (5.4): TE page 238; Transparencies
____ Warm-Up: Transparencies

TEACHING OPTIONS

____ Notetaking Guide
____ Examples: 1–4, SE pages 242–244
____ Extra Examples: TE pages 243–244
____ Your Turn Now Exercises: 1–10, SE pages 243–244
____ Concept Check: TE page 244
____ Getting Ready to Practice Exercises: 1–13, SE page 244

APPLY/HOMEWORK

Homework Assignment

____ Block Schedule: pp. 245–246 Exs. 16–25, 28–50, 52–57, 60–62

Reteaching the Lesson

____ Practice: CRB pages 42–44 (Level A, Level B, Level C); Practice Workbook
____ Study Guide: CRB pages 45–46; Spanish Study Guide

Extending the Lesson

____ Challenge: SE page 246; CRB page 47

ASSESSMENT OPTIONS

____ Daily Quiz (5.5): TE page 246 or Transparencies
____ Test-Taking Practice: SE page 246

Notes ____

____

____

Name ______________________________ Date __________

Practice A

For use with pages 242-246

Complete the statement.

1. A rational number is a number than can be written as $\frac{a}{b}$, where a and b are __________ and $b \neq$ ____.

2. A terminating decimal results if the quotient $\frac{a}{b}$ has a __________ of zero.

3. A __________ decimal results if the quotient $\frac{a}{b}$ has a digit or a group of digits that repeats without end.

Tell whether the number is included in each of the following number groups: *rational number, integer, whole number.*

4. 7 **5.** 0.431 **6.** -20 **7.** $0.\overline{136}$

Write the fraction or mixed number as a decimal.

8. $-\frac{2}{5}$ **9.** $\frac{1}{6}$ **10.** $\frac{23}{50}$ **11.** $-\frac{5}{12}$

12. $\frac{7}{16}$ **13.** $-2\frac{1}{2}$ **14.** $4\frac{8}{15}$ **15.** $3\frac{7}{9}$

16. $-\frac{23}{33}$ **17.** $\frac{15}{22}$ **18.** $-9\frac{9}{10}$ **19.** $-\frac{43}{45}$

Write the decimal as a fraction or mixed number.

20. 0.72 **21.** -0.45 **22.** 1.28 **23.** 2.65

24. $-0.13\overline{6}$ **25.** -0.6 **26.** $0.\overline{067}$ **27.** $0.\overline{284}$

In Exercises 28 and 29, order the numbers from least to greatest.

28. $\frac{1}{4}$, 0.2, $\frac{1}{3}$, $\frac{2}{7}$, 0.3

29. $4\frac{7}{8}$, 4.8, 4.9, $4\frac{3}{4}$, $4\frac{8}{9}$

30. The following distances in feet were the best long jumps of the 5 competitors at a track meet.

$15\frac{1}{4}$, $15\frac{2}{5}$, $14\frac{7}{8}$, $16\frac{1}{2}$, $15\frac{3}{5}$

Write the distances as decimals rounded to the nearest hundredth of a foot. Then order the values from least to greatest.

Lesson 5.5

LESSON 5.5

Name ____ Date ___________

Practice B

For use with pages 242–246

The diagram shows relationships between types of numbers. Tell which labeled area represents the given number type.

1. Whole numbers

2. Rational numbers

3. Integers

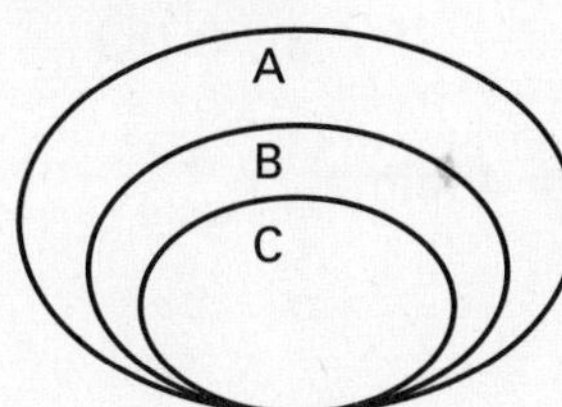

Tell whether the number is included in each of the following number groups: *rational number, integer, whole number.*

4. 16 **5.** 0.172 **6.** $0.\overline{27}$ **7.** −8

Write the fraction or mixed number as a decimal.

8. $\frac{3}{5}$ **9.** $-\frac{4}{9}$ **10.** $-\frac{9}{11}$ **11.** $\frac{11}{16}$

12. $3\frac{1}{8}$ **13.** $-5\frac{4}{27}$ **14.** $7\frac{16}{33}$ **15.** $\frac{33}{40}$

16. $-\frac{7}{100}$ **17.** $\frac{17}{34}$ **18.** $-8\frac{19}{50}$ **19.** $-\frac{70}{101}$

Write the decimal as a fraction or mixed number.

20. 0.24 **21.** −0.61 **22.** 2.48 **23.** 7.15

24. $-0.\overline{3}$ **25.** 0.95 **26.** $-0.\overline{124}$ **27.** −0.109

Order the numbers from least to greatest.

28. $\frac{6}{7}$, 0.8, $\frac{3}{4}$, $\frac{11}{13}$, 0.81

29. $6\frac{1}{5}$, 6.15, 6.3, $6\frac{1}{8}$, $6\frac{2}{19}$

In Exercises 30 and 31, use the table that shows the fraction of attempted passes that were completed by each quarterback one Sunday.

Warner	Collins	Griese	Garcia	Favre
$\frac{26}{39}$	$\frac{22}{26}$	$\frac{14}{20}$	$\frac{27}{36}$	$\frac{29}{44}$

30. Write each fraction as a decimal.

31. Write the names of the quarterbacks in order from the highest to lowest fractions of completed passes.

Lesson 5.5

LESSON **5.5**

Name ______________________________ Date __________

Practice C

For use with pages 242–246

Tell whether the number is included in each of the following number groups: *rational number, integer, whole number.*

1. 20 **2.** 0.64 **3.** $0.\overline{189}$ **4.** -19

Write the fraction or mixed number as a decimal.

5. $\frac{7}{8}$ **6.** $-\frac{10}{11}$ **7.** $-\frac{23}{66}$ **8.** $\frac{11}{32}$

9. $\frac{42}{75}$ **10.** $3\frac{5}{12}$ **11.** $7\frac{19}{60}$ **12.** $-8\frac{24}{32}$

13. $-1\frac{35}{84}$ **14.** $-2\frac{42}{55}$ **15.** $-\frac{28}{37}$ **16.** $-\frac{109}{200}$

Write the decimal as a fraction or a mixed number.

17. 0.35 **18.** -0.56 **19.** 1.68 **20.** 9.03

21. $-0.\overline{7}$ **22.** $0.1\overline{3}$ **23.** $-0.\overline{63}$ **24.** -2.245

In Exercises 25 and 26, order the numbers from least to greatest.

25. $\frac{12}{17}$, 0.75, $\frac{19}{25}$, $\frac{35}{44}$, 0.78 **26.** $7\frac{2}{5}$, 7.41, 7.48, $7\frac{8}{17}$, $7\frac{29}{38}$

27. Write the fractions $\frac{1}{9}$, $\frac{2}{9}$, and $\frac{3}{9}$ as decimals. Use your results to predict the decimal forms of $\frac{4}{9}$ and $\frac{7}{9}$.

In Exercises 28–30, use the table that shows the fraction of students at a middle school who participated in each school sport.

Sport	Football	Soccer	Volleyball	Basketball	Swimming
Fraction of Students	$\frac{3}{100}$	$\frac{7}{500}$	$\frac{3}{250}$	$\frac{3}{200}$	$\frac{1}{20}$

28. Write each fraction as a decimal and write the sports in order from greatest participation to least participation.

29. How many people participated in volleyball if there are 1000 students at the school?

30. How many more students played football than soccer if there are 1000 students at the school?

Lesson 5.5

Name ____________________ Date __________

Study Guide

For use with pages 242–246

GOAL Write fractions as decimals and decimals as fractions.

VOCABULARY

A **rational number** is a number that can be written as $\frac{a}{b}$, where a and b are integers and $b \neq 0$.

To write any rational number $\frac{a}{b}$ as a decimal, divide a by b. If the quotient has a remainder of zero, the result is a **terminating decimal.** If the quotient has a digit or group of digits that repeats without end, the result is a **repeating decimal.**

EXAMPLE 1 Writing Fractions as Decimals

To write a fraction as a decimal, divide the numerator by the denominator.

a. $\frac{4}{9} = 9\overline{)4.0000}$ = 0.4444...

$$\begin{array}{r} 0.4444... \\ 9\overline{)4.0000} \\ \underline{3\,6} \\ 40 \\ \underline{36} \\ 40 \\ \underline{36} \\ 40 \\ \underline{36} \\ 4 \end{array}$$

Answer: The quotient 0.444... is a repeating decimal. To indicate this, place a bar over the repeating digit: $\frac{4}{9} = 0.\overline{4}$.

b. $\frac{7}{8} = 8\overline{)7.000}$ = 0.875

$$\begin{array}{r} 0.875 \\ 8\overline{)7.000} \\ \underline{6\,4} \\ 60 \\ \underline{56} \\ 40 \\ \underline{40} \\ 0 \end{array}$$

Answer: The remainder is zero, so $\frac{7}{8} = 0.875$ is a terminating decimal.

EXAMPLE 2 Ordering Rational Numbers

Order the numbers from least to greatest.

$-3\frac{2}{5}, -3\frac{4}{5}, -3\frac{1}{6}, -3\frac{1}{3}$

Solution

Write the mixed numbers as decimals.

$-3\frac{2}{5} = -3.4$ $\quad -3\frac{4}{5} = -3.8$ $\quad -3\frac{1}{6} = -3.1\overline{6}$ $\quad -3\frac{1}{3} = -3.\overline{3}$

Answer: The numbers in order from least to greatest are:

$-3\frac{4}{5}, -3\frac{2}{5}, -3\frac{1}{3}$, and $-3\frac{1}{6}$.

Lesson 5.5

Name ______________________ Date ________

Study Guide

For use with pages 242–246

Exercises for Examples 1 and 2

Write the fraction as a decimal.

1. $\frac{5}{6}$ **2.** $\frac{7}{15}$ **3.** $\frac{9}{11}$

Order the numbers from least to greatest.

4. $1\frac{1}{2}, 1\frac{2}{7}, 1\frac{5}{12}, 1.3, 1.1$ **5.** $-\frac{1}{5}, -\frac{3}{8}, -\frac{7}{18}\ -0.4, -0.3$

EXAMPLE 3 Writing Terminating Decimals as Fractions

Write the decimal as a fraction or mixed number.

a. 0.8

$0.8 = \frac{8}{10}$ 8 is in the tenths place.

$= \frac{4}{5}$

b. −3.25

$-3.25 = -3\frac{25^{1}}{100_{4}}$ 5 is in the hundredths place.

$= -3\frac{1}{4}$

EXAMPLE 4 Writing Repeating Decimals as Fractions

To write $0.\overline{27}$ as a fraction, let $x = 0.\overline{27}$ or 0.272727….

(1) The number has 2 repeating digits, so multiply by 100. So, $100x = 27.272727\ldots$.

(2) Then subtract x from $100x$.

$$100x = 27.272727\ldots$$
$$-x = -0.272727\ldots$$
$$99x = 27$$

(3) Solve for x. Simplify. $x = \frac{27}{99}$ or $\frac{3}{11}$

Answer: The decimal $0.\overline{27}$ is equivalent to the fraction $\frac{3}{11}$.

Exercises for Examples 3 and 4

Write the decimal as a fraction or mixed number.

6. 0.75 **7.** 4.003 **8.** −2.36

9. $0.\overline{5}$ **10.** $0.\overline{36}$ **11.** $0.\overline{19}$

Lesson 5.5

Name ______________________ Date __________

Challenge Practice

For use with pages 242–246

In Exercises 1–4, use the table at the right.

Fraction	Decimal
$\frac{1}{7}$	
$\frac{2}{7}$	
$\frac{3}{7}$	
$\frac{4}{7}$	
$\frac{5}{7}$	
$\frac{6}{7}$	

1. Complete the table by writing each fraction as a repeating decimal number.
2. Describe the similarity in the pattern of repeating digits.
3. The fraction $\frac{2}{7}$ can be written as $2 \cdot \frac{1}{7}$, or $2 \cdot (0.\overline{142857})$ as shown below.

$$\begin{array}{r} 0.\overline{142857} \\ \times \quad\quad\quad 2 \\ \hline 0.\overline{285714} \end{array}$$

Show how this relationship is true for the fraction $\frac{6}{7}$.

4. Use the fact that $\frac{1}{13} = 0.\overline{076923}$ to write $\frac{5}{13}$ as a repeating decimal without dividing.

In Exercises 5–7, write the fraction as a decimal. *(Hint:* Continue dividing until the pattern repeats.)

5. $\frac{1}{17}$

6. $\frac{1}{19}$

7. $\frac{1}{23}$

8. Use your results from Exercises 5–7 to make a conjecture about the maximum number of digits possible in the repeating pattern when writing a fraction as a decimal.
9. Use an example to show why your conjecture in Exercise 8 only applies to the maximum number of digits, not necessarily to the exact number of digits.

LESSON 5.6

Teacher's Name ____________________ Class ______ Room ______ Date ______

Lesson Plan

1-day lesson (See *Pacing and Assignment Guide*, TE page 216A)

For use with pages 247–250

GOAL **Add and subtract decimals.**

State/Local Objectives ____

Lesson 5.6

✓ Check the items you wish to use for this lesson.

STARTING OPTIONS

____ Homework Check (5.5): TE page 245; Answer Transparencies
____ Homework Quiz (5.5): TE page 246; Transparencies
____ Warm-Up Transparencies

TEACHING OPTIONS

____ Notetaking Guide
____ Examples: 1–3, SE pages 247–248
____ Extra Examples: TE page 248
____ Your Turn Now Exercises: 1–11, SE pages 247–248
____ Concept Check: TE page 248
____ Getting Ready to Practice Exercises: 1–10, SE page 249

APPLY/HOMEWORK

Homework Assignment

____ Basic: SRH p. 709 Exs. 9–12; pp. 249–250 Exs. 13–24, 29–31, 35–37, 39–42, 48–56
____ Average: pp. 249–250 Exs. 17–28, 32–43, 48–57
____ Advanced: pp. 249–250 Exs. 21–28, 32–47*, 50–57

Reteaching the Lesson

____ Practice: CRB pages 50–52 (Level A, Level B, Level C); Practice Workbook
____ Study Guide: CRB pages 53–54; Spanish Study Guide

Extending the Lesson

____ Real-World Problem Solving: CRB page 55
____ Challenge: SE page 250; CRB page 56

ASSESSMENT OPTIONS

____ Daily Quiz (5.6): TE page 250 or Transparencies
____ Test-Taking Practice: SE page 250

Notes ____

Teacher's Name ______________________ Class ______ Room ______ Date ______

Lesson Plan for Block Scheduling

Half-block lesson (See *Pacing and Assignment Guide*, TE page 216A)

For use with pages 247–250

GOAL **Add and subtract decimals.**

State/Local Objectives ____

____

✓ Check the items you wish to use for this lesson.

Chapter Pacing Guide	
Day	**Lesson**
1	5.1; 5.2
2	5.3; 5.4
3	5.5
4	**5.6;** 5.7 (begin)
5	5.7 (end); 5.8
6	Ch. 5 Review and Projects

STARTING OPTIONS

____ Homework Check (5.5): TE page 245; Answer Transparencies
____ Homework Quiz (5.5): TE page 246; Transparencies
____ Warm-Up: Transparencies

TEACHING OPTIONS

____ Notetaking Guide
____ Examples: 1–3, SE pages 247–248
____ Extra Examples: TE page 248
____ Your Turn Now Exercises: 1–11, SE pages 247–248
____ Concept Check: TE page 248
____ Getting Ready to Practice Exercises: 1–10, SE page 249

APPLY/HOMEWORK

Homework Assignment

____ Block Schedule: pp. 249–250 Exs. 17–28, 32–43, 48–57 (with 5.7)

Reteaching the Lesson

____ Practice: CRB pages 50–52 (Level A, Level B, Level C); Practice Workbook
____ Study Guide: CRB pages 53–54; Spanish Study Guide

Extending the Lesson

____ Real-World Problem Solving: CRB page 55
____ Challenge: SE page 250; CRB page 56

ASSESSMENT OPTIONS

____ Daily Quiz (5.6): TE page 250 or Transparencies
____ Test-Taking Practice: SE page 250

Notes ____

____

____

Name ______________________________ Date __________

Practice A

For use with pages 247–250

Match the expression with its solution.

1. $7.51 + 3.68$ **A.** 11.02

2. $-4.26 + 15.7$ **B.** 11.19

3. $1.093 + 9.927$ **C.** 11.44

4. $36.42 - 24.67$ **D.** 11.75

Find the sum or difference.

5. $7.64 + 13.072$ **6.** $3.112 + 0.249$ **7.** $-8.07 + 1.965$

8. $-0.45 + (-1.2)$ **9.** $9.1 + (-2.637)$ **10.** $-13.64 + 1.364$

11. $-5.26 - 0.705$ **12.** $36.2 - (-7.49)$ **13.** $19.822 - 4.7$

14. $1.68 - 8.2$ **15.** $14.3 - (-5.9)$ **16.** $-0.88 - 0.204$

Solve the equation.

17. $w + 2.6 = 41$ **18.** $-1.89 + x = 3.64$ **19.** $z - 3.4 = 15.21$

20. $a + 8.05 = 8.91$ **21.** $m + (-6.45) = -13.78$ **22.** $-12.43 + p = -15.26$

In Exercises 23–26, use front-end estimation to estimate the sum.

23. $7.18 + 9.33 + 1.08 + 12.99$ **24.** $15.06 + 23.94 + 3.11 + 26.75$

25. $19.37 + 2.08 + 24.09 + 33.66$ **26.** $27.10 + 39.61 + 49.22 + 1.07$

27. Your bill at a restaurant comes to a total of \$13.95. You leave a \$2.50 tip. How much money did you spend at the restaurant?

In Exercises 28–30, find the perimeter of the figure.

28.

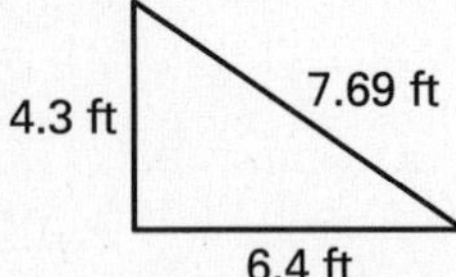

29.

15.1 in.

2.99 in. 2.99 in.

15.1 in.

30.

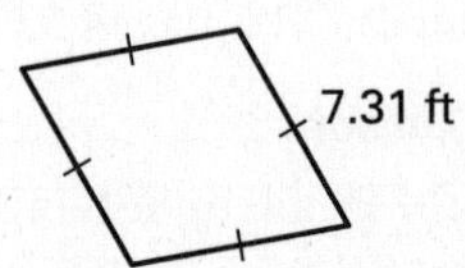

31. Describe and correct the error in the solution.

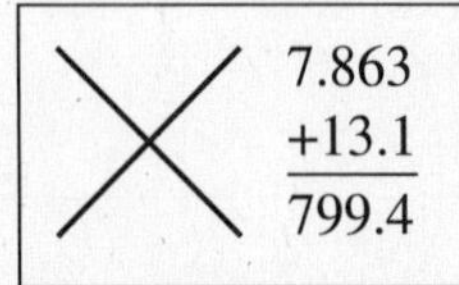

32. For dinner you are making jambalaya. You need 3.5 pounds of chicken and 1.25 pounds of sausage. How many pounds of meat are you using in this dish?

LESSON 5.6

Name ______________________________ Date __________

Practice B

For use with pages 247-250

Find the sum or difference.

1. $6.41 + 12.893$ **2.** $0.37 + 1.498$ **3.** $-7.25 + 3.704$

4. $-0.78 + (-2.8)$ **5.** $8.2 + (-4.516)$ **6.** $-22.115 + 2.67$

7. $-9.54 - 0.068$ **8.** $37.24 - (-6.518)$ **9.** $24.669 - 8.1$

10. $1.45 - 7.3$ **11.** $25.26 - (-11.047)$ **12.** $-0.935 - 0.14$

Solve the equation.

13. $f + 5.3 = 36$ **14.** $-2.64 + g = 5.17$ **15.** $h - 9.21 = 13.8$

16. $j + 0.545 = 18.23$ **17.** $k + (-9.32) = -10.764$ **18.** $-8.54 + m = -23.612$

In Exercises 19–22, use front-end estimation to estimate the sum.

19. $7.612 + 5.93 + 2.87 + 14.11$ **20.** $20.94 + 12.06 + 13.88 + 17.354$

21. $34.25 + 18.34 + 2.994 + 42.068$ **22.** $42.87 + 31.652 + 11.0258 + 46.35$

23. This month, Sara had a phone bill that was \$43.15, a cable bill that was \$35.87, and an electric bill that was \$56.23. What was the total of the 3 bills?

In Exercises 24–26, find the perimeter of the figure.

24.

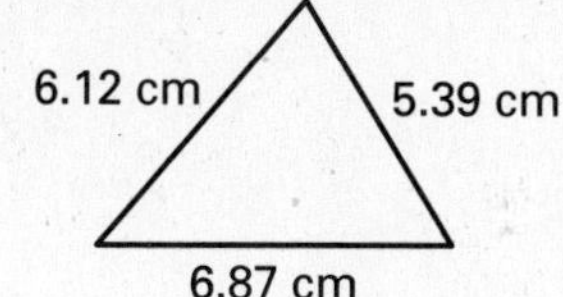

25.

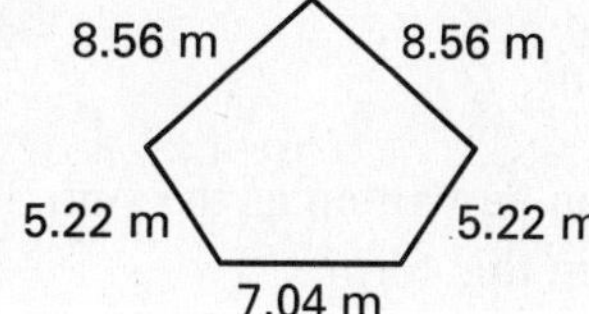

26.

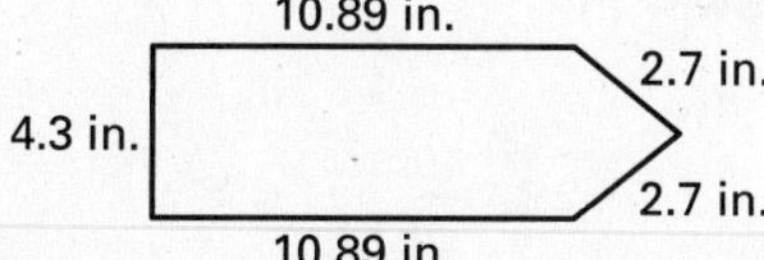

27. The number 18.34 can be written as the sum $10 + 8 + 0.3 + 0.04$. Write 175.9231 as a sum in this form.

In Exercises 28–30, use the following information. You need 4.625 yards of fabric to make a dress. You also want to make a matching jacket that requires 2.5 yards of the same fabric.

28. How many yards of fabric will you need to make both pieces?

29. If the store only had one bolt with 7.05 yards of fabric on the bolt, is there enough fabric for you to purchase?

30. What is the difference between what you need and what the store has available?

Name ______________________________ Date __________

Practice C

For use with pages 247–250

Find the sum or difference.

1. 5.43 + 23.026 **2.** 1.774 + 0.528 **3.** −9.13 + 2.604

4. −0.61 + (−3.895) **5.** 10.003 + 7.62 **6.** −8.91 − 0.654

7. 31.29 − (−12.65) **8.** 17.8 − 3.631 **9.** 1.93 − 12.47

10. 1.85 + (−9.2) **11.** 27.8 − (−4.616) **12.** −0.714 − 0.369

Lesson 5.6

Solve the equation.

13. $a + 3.81 = 23$ **14.** $-6.49 + b = 17.82$ **15.** $-1.093 + c = 3.84$

16. $d - 4.72 = 1.61$ **17.** $e + (-12.013) = -2.685$ **18.** $-9.867 + f = -13.143$

Use front-end estimation to estimate the sum.

19. 2.981 + 3.4 + 19.55 + 14.56 **20.** 12.15 + 35.48 + 49.65 + 11.58

21. 24.89 + 16.97 +2.48 + 37.56 **22.** 7.89 + 7.14 + 6.99 + 4.87 + 7.58

In Exercises 23 and 24, find the perimeter of the figure.

23.

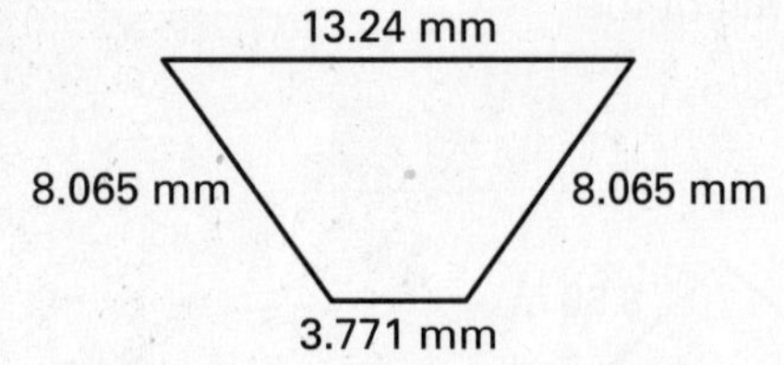

24.

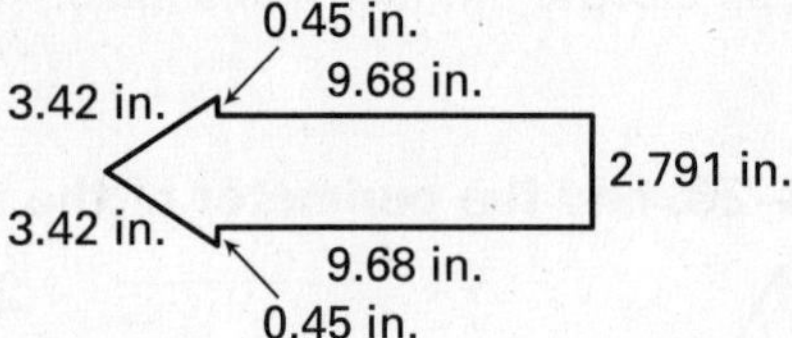

25. The number 32.58 can be written as the sum 30 + 2 + 0.5 + 0.08. Write 2984.5713 as a sum in this form.

In Exercises 26–29, find the sum or difference. Write your answer in decimal form.

26. $7.19 + \frac{15}{4}$ **27.** $\frac{4}{5} - 1.38$ **28.** $16.09 - \frac{24}{10}$ **29.** $\frac{19}{20} + 1.658$

30. David did 4 errands and drove a total of 52.94 miles. The trip to the grocery store was 8.16 miles. The trip to the bank was 11.33 miles. Driving to the book store was another 15.5 miles. How many miles did he drive to do the last errand?

31. Claire received a score of 82.56 after playing a game, and Madison received a score of 84.2 after playing the same game. How much higher was Madison's score than Claire's?

Name ______________________ Date __________

Study Guide

For use with pages 247–250

GOAL Add and subtract decimals.

VOCABULARY

Front-end estimation can be used to estimate sums. Add the front-end digits to get a low estimate. Then use the remaining digits to adjust the sum to a closer estimate.

Lesson 5.6

EXAMPLE 1 Adding and Subtracting Decimals

a. You make a mixture using the same amount of each kind of nut. The fat in 2 tablespoons of peanuts is 8.92 grams and in 2 tablespoons of pecans is 9.1 grams. Find the total amount of fat in a 4 tablespoon serving of the mixture.

$$\begin{array}{r} 8.92 \\ +9.10 \\ \hline 18.02 \end{array}$$ ← Use a zero as a placeholder.

Answer: There are 18.02 grams of fat in the mixture.

b. How many more grams of fat per serving are there in pecans than in peanuts?

$$\begin{array}{r} 9.10 \\ -8.92 \\ \hline 0.18 \end{array}$$ ← Use a zero as a placeholder.

Answer: There is 0.18 gram more fat in pecans than in peanuts.

Exercises for Example 1

Find the sum or difference.

1. $-13.2 + (-6.02)$

2. $8.72 + 0.461$

3. $5.21 - 3.651$

4. $3.329 - (-0.3)$

EXAMPLE 2 Solving Equations with Decimals

a.

$x + (-0.79) = 3.6$	Write original equation.
$x + (-0.79) + 0.79 = 3.6 + 0.79$	Add 0.79 to each side to undo adding -0.79.
$x = 4.39$	Simplify.

b.

$y - 2.817 = 8.52$	Write original equation.
$y - 2.817 + 2.817 = 8.52 + 2.817$	Add to undo subtraction.
$y = 11.337$	Simplify.

Name ______________________ Date __________

Study Guide

For use with pages 247–250

Exercises for Example 2

Solve the equation.

5. $x + 2.3 = 4.9$

6. $y + (-9.4) = 14.77$

7. $z - 10.1 = 25.9$

8. $x - (-8.8) = 16.91$

Lesson 5.6

EXAMPLE 3 Using Front-End Estimation

Estimate the total cost of 4 items priced at \$2.39, \$1.75, \$2.56, and \$4.30.

Solution

Use front-end estimation.

(1) Add the **front-end digits**: the dollars.

(2) Estimate the sum of the remaining digits: the cents.

(3) Add your results.

(1)	(2)		(3)
\$**2**.39	\$2.**39**		\$9
\$**1**.75	\$1.**75**	**\$1**	+\$2
\$**2**.56	\$2.**56**	**\$1**	\$11
\$**4**.30	\$4.**30**		
\$9		**\$2**	

Answer: The estimated cost of the 4 items is \$11.

Exercises for Example 3

Use front-end estimation to estimate the sum.

9. \$6.43 + \$6.05 + \$5.95 + \$6.59

10. 15.41 + 16 + 15.92 + 16.62 + 16.21

Name ______________________________ Date __________

Real-World Problem Solving

For use with pages 247–250

Yard Sales

Many people like to have yard sales to sell off old or unwanted items. Yard sales are a way to be outside, do a little socializing, and make a few dollars on things you no longer need.

In Exercises 1–3, use the following information.

Amanda's family was participating in a neighborhood yard sale. Amanda went through her clothes and personal items to sort out things she no longer needed. She put prices on all her things and labeled them with an "A." As her mother sold Amanda's things, she would put the label in a column marked "Amanda," and they would add up the total later. At first, Amanda was excited to help her mom with the yard sale. After a while, she became bored. She wanted to go see what other people had for sale. Her mom gave her $1.00 and marked it down in Amanda's column. A little later, the ice cream truck came by, and Amanda borrowed $.75 from her mom to buy ice cream. By the end of the day, this is what Amanda's column looked like:

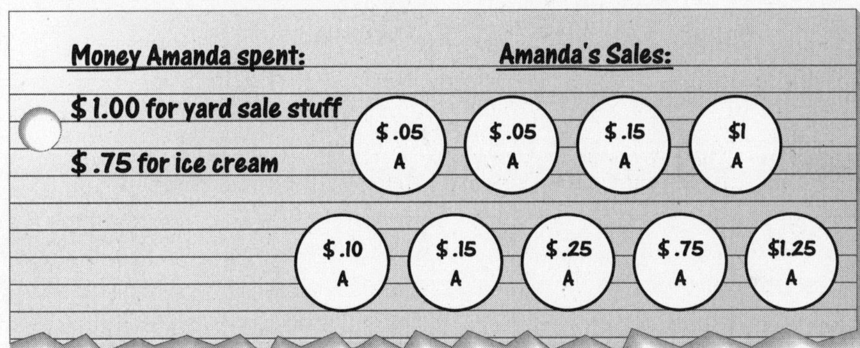

1. Add up all of Amanda's labels. How much money did she make from her sales?
2. Add up the money Amanda spent. How much money did she spend?
3. Subtract the money Amanda spent from the money she earned. What is the total amount of money Amanda had left?
4. Amanda is going to try to sell more things the next day. Write and solve an equation to find the amount of money Amanda needs to earn on day 2 to give her total earnings of $10.

Lesson 5.6

Name ______________________________ Date __________

Challenge Practice

For use with pages 247-250

Simplify the expression.

1. $[-32.79 + (4.23 - 18.25)] - 8.15$

2. $[-12.35 - (6.34 + 5.72)] + 18.125$

3. $(-3.167 - 12.249) - \left(\frac{4}{5} - 2\frac{1}{10}\right)$

4. $-10.585 - [(12.482 - 4.999) - (-5.735 - 8.34)]$

5. $|-9.6 - (3.5 - 12.6)|$

Lesson 5.6

In Exercises 6–9, find the sum or difference of the repeating decimal numbers.

Example: $0.\overline{18} + 0.\overline{2}$

$0.\overline{18} + 0.\overline{22}$ Write the decimals to the same decimal place.

$0.\overline{40}$ Add the decimals.

6. $0.\overline{34} - 0.\overline{12}$

7. $0.\overline{4} + 0.\overline{352}$

8. $-0.\overline{45} - 0.\overline{3}$

9. $0.\overline{032} + (-0.\overline{75})$

10. Verify that the difference you found in Exercise 8 is correct by writing the decimals as fractions, finding the difference, and then writing the answer in decimal form.

LESSON 5.7

Teacher's Name ____________________ Class ______ Room ______ Date ______

Lesson Plan

2-day lesson (See *Pacing and Assignment Guide*, TE page 216A)

For use with pages 251–254

GOAL **Multiply and divide decimals.**

State/Local Objectives ____________________

____

✓ **Check the items you wish to use for this lesson.**

STARTING OPTIONS

____ Homework Check (5.6): TE page 249; Answer Transparencies
____ Homework Quiz (5.6): TE page 250; Transparencies
____ Warm-Up Transparencies

TEACHING OPTIONS

____ Notetaking Guide
____ Examples: Day 1: 1, SE page 251; Day 2: 2–3, SE page 252
____ Extra Examples: TE page 252
____ Your Turn Now Exercises: Day 1: 1–4, SE page 251; Day 2: 5–10, SE page 252
____ Concept Check: TE page 252
____ Getting Ready to Practice Exercises: Day 1: 2–3, 6, SE page 253; Day 2: 1, 4–5, SE page 253

APPLY/HOMEWORK

Homework Assignment

____ Basic: Day 1: SRH p. 714 Exs. 6–10; pp. 253–254 Exs. 7–14, 24, 27–29, 37–41
Day 2: SRH p. 715 Exs. 6–10; pp. 253–254 Exs. 15–22, 26, 30–32, 42–46
____ Average: Day 1: pp. 253–254 Exs. 7–14, 23–28, 37–42
Day 2: pp. 253–254 Exs. 15–22, 29–35, 43–47
____ Advanced: Day 1: pp. 253–254 Exs. 7–14, 23–28, 37–41
Day 2: pp. 253–254 Exs. 15–22, 29–36*, 45–47

Reteaching the Lesson

____ Practice: CRB pages 59–61 (Level A, Level B, Level C); Practice Workbook
____ Study Guide: CRB pages 62–63; Spanish Study Guide

Extending the Lesson

____ Challenge: SE page 254; CRB page 64

ASSESSMENT OPTIONS

____ Daily Quiz (5.7): TE page 254 or Transparencies
____ Test-Taking Practice: SE page 254

Notes ____________________

____

____

LESSON 5.7

Teacher's Name ____________________ Class ______ Room ________ Date ________

Lesson Plan for Block Scheduling

1-block lesson (See *Pacing and Assignment Guide*, TE page 216A)

For use with pages 251–254

GOAL **Multiply and divide decimals.**

State/Local Objectives ____

____

✓ **Check the items you wish to use for this lesson.**

Chapter Pacing Guide	
Day	**Lesson**
1	5.1; 5.2
2	5.3; 5.4
3	5.5
4	5.6; **5.7 (begin)**
5	**5.7 (end)**; 5.8
6	Ch. 5 Review and Projects

STARTING OPTIONS

____ Homework Check (5.6): TE page 249; Answer Transparencies
____ Homework Quiz (5.6): TE page 250; Transparencies
____ Warm-Up: Transparencies

TEACHING OPTIONS

____ Notetaking Guide
____ Examples: Day 4: 1, SE page 251; Day 5: 2–3, SE page 252
____ Extra Examples: TE page 252
____ Your Turn Now Exercises: Day 4: 1–4, SE page 251; Day 5: 5–10, SE page 252
____ Concept Check: TE page 252
____ Getting Ready to Practice Exercises: Day 4: 2–3, 6, SE page 253; Day 5: 1, 4–5, SE page 253

Lesson 5.7

APPLY/HOMEWORK

Homework Assignment

____ Block Schedule: Day 4: pp. 253–254 Exs. 7–14, 23–28, 37–42 (with 5.6)
Day 5: pp. 253–254 Exs. 15–22, 29–35, 43–47 (with 5.8)

Reteaching the Lesson

____ Practice: CRB pages 59–61 (Level A, Level B, Level C); Practice Workbook
____ Study Guide: CRB pages 62–63; Spanish Study Guide

Extending the Lesson

____ Challenge: SE page 254; CRB page 64

ASSESSMENT OPTIONS

____ Daily Quiz (5.7): TE page 254 or Transparencies
____ Test-Taking Practice: SE page 254

Notes ____

____

____

LESSON 5.7

Name ______________________________ Date __________

Practice A

For use with pages 251–254

Complete the statement.

1. When multiplying decimals, the number of decimal places in the __________ is the total number of decimal places in the __________.

2. The __________ is the leftmost nonzero digit.

Tell which label shows the given part of the division problem.

3. quotient

4. dividend

5. divisor

A. → 2.75

B. → 6.4)17.6 ← C.

Find the product or the quotient.

6. 15×0.4	**7.** 6.1×2.8	**8.** $1.9 \times (-0.5)$
9. $6.4 \div 0.8$	**10.** $14.4 \div 0.12$	**11.** $9.02 \div (-0.2)$
12. $19.33 \times (-4.75)$	**13.** $-8.145 \div (-5.43)$	**14.** $30.6735 \div 7.5$
15. $19.1186 \div 1.09$	**16.** 0.0695×2.113	**17.** $3.0408 \div 0.084$

In Exercises 18–20, use the following information. A basketball court is 15.3 meters wide and 28.7 meters long. What is the area of the basketball court?

18. Write a verbal model for the problem.

19. Substitute the given values and solve.

20. Check to see that your answer is reasonable.

21. There are 3.25 grams of protein in an ounce of cottage cheese. How much protein is there in a 4.6 ounce serving of cottage cheese?

Solve the equation.

22. $-16.9 = -1.3x$	**23.** $7.3w = 47.45$	**24.** $\frac{m}{1.81} = 9.7$
25. $\frac{g}{-0.065} = 11.28$	**26.** $0.047y = -0.67633$	**27.** $\frac{z}{17.17} = 2.43$

Lesson 5.7

Name ______________________________ Date __________

Practice B

For use with pages 251–254

In Exercises 1–3, place the labels of the steps for dividing decimals in order.

1. _____

2. _____

3. _____

A. Place the decimal point in the quotient so that it lines up with the decimal point in the dividend.

B. Divide.

C. Multiply both the divisor and the dividend by the power of ten that will make the divisor a whole number.

Find the product or the quotient.

4. 8×0.32

5. 7.4×9.1

6. $2.56 \times (-0.7)$

7. $7.2 \div 0.8$

8. $3.675 \div 0.15$

9. $11.26 \div (-0.4)$

10. $24.38 \times (-7.11)$

11. $-26.7804 \div (-6.92)$

12. $115.425 \div 8.1$

13. $12.104 \div 13.6$

14. 0.00075×15.2

15. $54.76 \div 7.4$

Lesson 5.7

In Exercises 16–18, use the following information. The Taj Mahal is a building in Agra, India, that was built by an emperor in memory of his wife. Around the building are rectangular gardens that are 0.305 kilometer wide and 0.305 kilometer long. What is the area of the gardens around the Taj Mahal?

16. Write a verbal model to describe the problem.

17. Substitute the given values and solve.

18. Check to see that your answer is reasonable.

In Exercises 19–24, solve the equation.

19. $-19.95 = -3.2x$

20. $8.1w = 7.29$

21. $\frac{m}{2.41} = 6.6$

22. $\frac{g}{-0.0054} = 12.9$

23. $0.037y = -0.94128$

24. $\frac{z}{22.14} = 1.07$

25. You have 5.375 pounds of hamburger for a cookout. You want to make quarter-pound (0.25 pound) hamburger patties. How many patties are you able to make with the meat that you have?

26. You have a photograph that measures 3.5 inches by 6.5 inches. What is the area of the photograph?

In Exercises 27–29, evaluate the expression.

27. $1.3^2 + 3.4 - 6.4 \div 0.8$

28. $1.69 \div (1.8 - 0.5) + 2.7$

29. $5.25 - 4.73 + 6.1^2$

30. You want to mail a first class letter. The cost is \$.37 for the first ounce and \$.23 for every ounce after that. How much will it cost to mail a letter that weighs 15 ounces?

Name ______________________________ Date __________

Practice C

For use with pages 251–254

In Exercises 1–12, find the product or the quotient.

1. 14×0.18 **2.** 3.95×2.6 **3.** $7.15 \times (-2.3)$

4. $9.502 \div 2.5$ **5.** 0.00325×20.9 **6.** $38.34 \div 7.1$

7. $12.4 \div 0.6$ **8.** $8.225 \div 0.15$ **9.** $36.774 \div (-6.81)$

10. $30.4512 \times (-4.16)$ **11.** $-91.5624 \div (-7.29)$ **12.** $29.181 \div 4.26$

13. A postage stamp is 1.875 inches wide. If a roll of stamps is printed so that the stamps are side by side, how many stamps are on a roll that is 46.875 inches long?

14. A *butcher block* of wood is made up of many lengths of boards glued together. You want to make a table top that is 63.75 inches wide out of butcher block. The boards you are using are 1.875 inches wide. How many boards wide will your butcher block table top be?

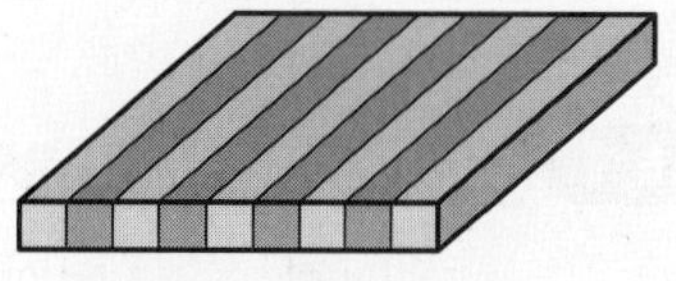
"Butcher Block"

15. Rather than build a picket fence along the side edge of your yard, you are planting bushes that will grow together to make a natural hedge. Each bush is expected to grow to be 3.25 feet wide. If the side of your yard is 168 feet, how many bushes should you buy? You decide to use the hedges to enclose your backyard for your dog. If your yard and house have the dimensions shown, how many more bushes should you buy?

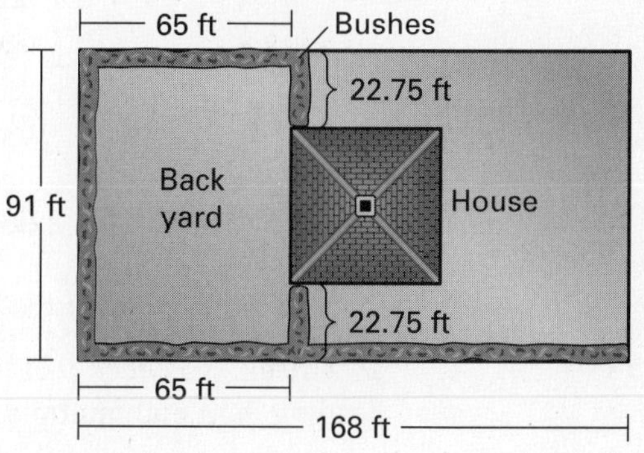

Solve the equation.

16. $-52.736 = -6.4a$ **17.** $0.0295b = -0.45371$ **18.** $\frac{c}{16.49} = 3.57$

Evaluate the expression.

19. $7.1^2 - 6.4 \div 0.8 + 1.9$

20. $4.5 + 3.6 \div (9.83 - 8.63)$

21. $5.2^2 + (3.7 - 2.8) \times 4.1$

Lesson 5.7

LESSON 5.7

Name ______________________ Date __________

Study Guide

For use with pages 251–254

GOAL Multiply and divide decimals.

VOCABULARY

Multiplying Decimals

Multiply decimals as you do whole numbers. Then place the decimal point. The number of decimal places in the product is the total number of decimal places in the factors.

A number's **leading digit** is its leftmost nonzero digit. To check that a product is reasonable, round each factor to its leading digit and multiply.

Dividing Decimals

When you divide by a decimal, multiply both the divisor and the dividend by the power of 10 that will make the divisor an integer. Then divide.

EXAMPLE 1 Multiplying Decimals

A rectangle has a length of 27.3 centimeters and a width of 18.8 centimeters. Find the area of the rectangle.

```
  27.3        1 decimal place
× 18.8      + 1 decimal place
  2184
 2184
 273
 513.24       2 decimal places
```

Answer: The area of the rectangle is 513.24 square centimeters.

✓ **Check:** To check that the product is reasonable, round each factor to its leading digit and multiply. $30 \times 20 = 600$ ✓

Exercises for Example 1

Multiply. Show that your answer is reasonable.

1. -6.31×4.5

2. 18.27×6.01

3. -0.81×11

4. $-0.23 \times (-0.5)$

LESSON 5.7 Continued

Name ______________________________ Date __________

Study Guide

For use with pages 251–254

EXAMPLE 2 Dividing Decimals

To divide 14.95 by 6.5, multiply the divisor and dividend by 10. Move the decimal points 1 place to the right.

$6.5\overline{)14.95}$ Move decimal points. Then divide.

$$\begin{array}{r} 2.3 \\ 65.\overline{)149.5} \\ \underline{130} \\ 19\,5 \\ \underline{19\,5} \\ 0 \end{array}$$

✓ **Check:** To check that the quotient is reasonable, round the quotient and the original divisor to the leading digit. Then multiply. The result should be close in value to the dividend.

2.3×6.5 round $\Rightarrow$ $2 \times 7 = 14$ ✓

Exercises for Example 2

Find the quotient.

5. $26.66 \div 8.6$

6. $2.645 \div 2.3$

7. $0.7 \div 0.5$

8. $13.3245 \div 5.67$

Lesson 5.7

EXAMPLE 3 Using Zeros as Placeholders

To find some quotients, you may need to use zeros as placeholders.

Placeholder in Dividend

$8 \div 2.5$

$2.5\overline{)8.0}$ ← zero as placeholder

$$\begin{array}{r} 3.2 \\ 25\overline{)80.0} \\ \underline{75} \\ 5\,0 \\ \underline{5\,0} \\ 0 \end{array}$$

Placeholder in Quotient

$0.2816 \div 6.4$

$6.4\overline{)0.2816}$ zero as placeholder

$$\begin{array}{r} 0.044 \\ 64\overline{)2.816} \\ \underline{2\,56} \\ 256 \\ \underline{256} \\ 0 \end{array}$$

Exercises for Example 3

Find the quotient.

9. $0.5 \div 3.2$

10. $0.1664 \div 0.8$

Name ______________________________ Date __________

Challenge Practice

For use with pages 251–254

In Exercises 1–4, use the formula to find the area of the figure.

1. $A = \frac{1}{2}bh$

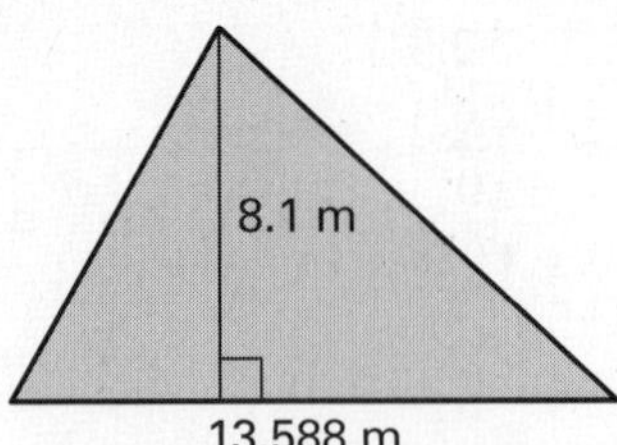

2. $A = 3.14r^2$

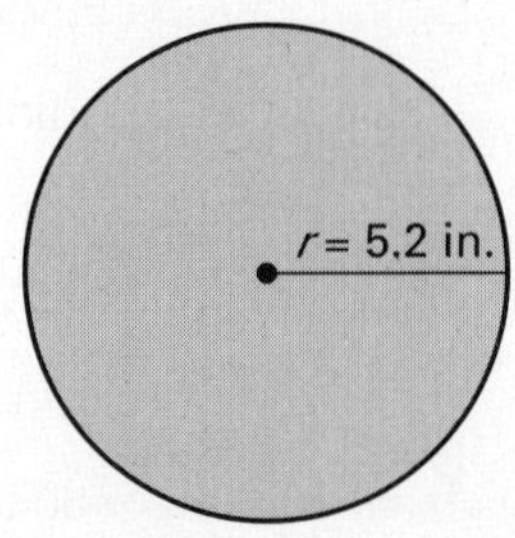

3. $A = \frac{1}{2}(b_1 + b_2)h$

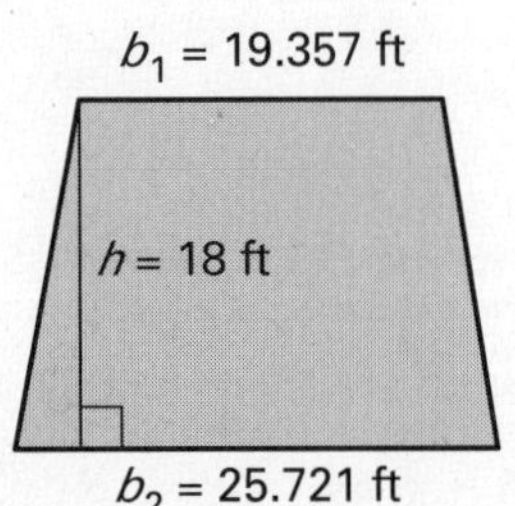

4. $A = bh$

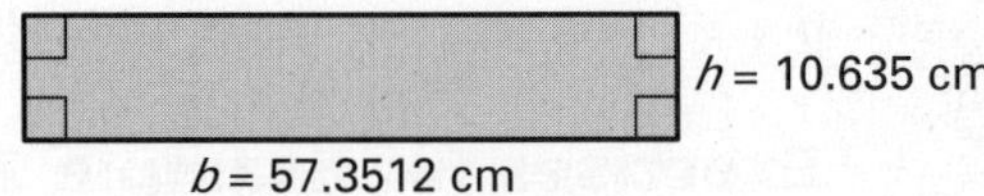

In Exercises 5 and 6, use the formula to find the missing dimension of the figure.

5. Volume of a cylinder = 284.641 mm^3
$V = 3.14r^2h$

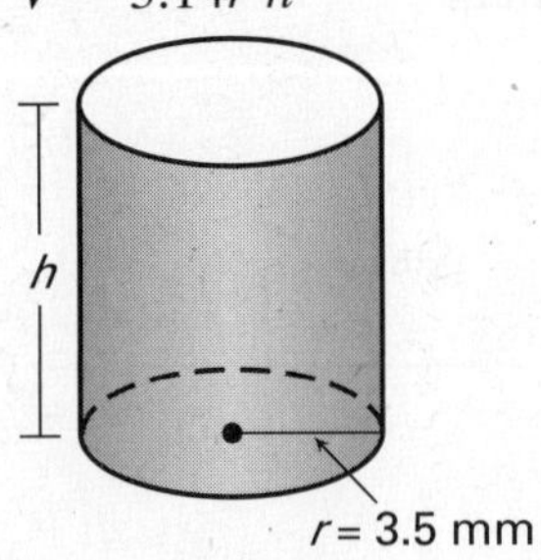

6. Volume of a rectangular prism = 668.98 $in.^3$
$V = \ell wh$

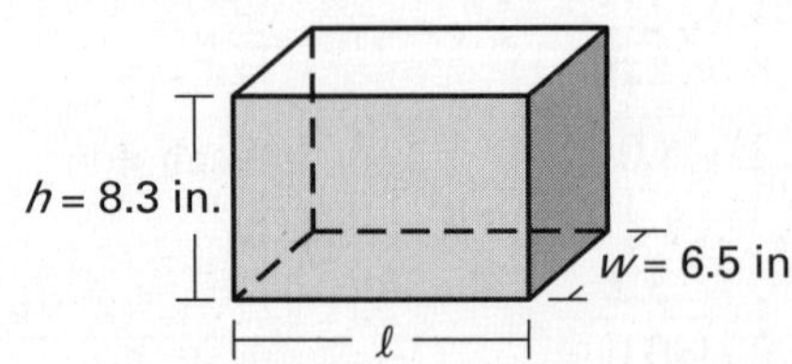

LESSON 5.8

Teacher's Name ______________________ Class ______ Room ______ Date ______

Lesson Plan

1-day lesson (See *Pacing and Assignment Guide*, TE page 216A)

For use with pages 255–261

GOAL **Describe data sets using mean, median, mode, and range.**

State/Local Objectives ____

____

✓ Check the items you wish to use for this lesson.

STARTING OPTIONS

____ Homework Check (5.7): TE page 253; Answer Transparencies
____ Homework Quiz (5.7): TE page 254; Transparencies
____ Warm-Up Transparencies

TEACHING OPTIONS

____ Notetaking Guide
____ Hands-on Activity: SE pages 255–256
____ Examples: 1–3, SE pages 257–258
____ Extra Examples: TE page 258
____ Your Turn Now Exercises: 1–4, SE pages 257–258
____ Technology Activity with Keystrokes: CRB pages 67–68
____ Concept Check: TE page 258
____ Getting Ready to Practice Exercises: 1–7, SE page 259

APPLY/HOMEWORK

Homework Assignment

____ Basic: pp. 259–261 Exs. 8–15, 17–19, 24–34
____ Average: pp. 259–261 Exs. 10–22, 24–34
____ Advanced: pp. 259–261 Exs. 10–25*, 28–34

Reteaching the Lesson

____ Practice: CRB pages 69–71 (Level A, Level B, Level C); Practice Workbook
____ Study Guide: CRB pages 72–73; Spanish Study Guide

Extending the Lesson

____ Challenge: SE page 260; CRB page 74

ASSESSMENT OPTIONS

____ Daily Quiz (5.8): TE page 261 or Transparencies
____ Test-Taking Practice: SE page 261
____ Quiz (5.5–5.8): SE page 263; Assessment Book page 58

Notes ____

____

____

LESSON 5.8

Teacher's Name ________________________ Class ______ Room _______ Date_______

Lesson Plan for Block Scheduling

Half-block lesson (See *Pacing and Assignment Guide*, TE page 216A)

For use with pages 255–261

GOAL **Describe data sets using mean, median, mode, and range.**

State/Local Objectives ____

____

✓ Check the items you wish to use for this lesson.

Chapter Pacing Guide	
Day	**Lesson**
1	5.1; 5.2
2	5.3; 5.4
3	5.5
4	5.6; 5.7 (begin)
5	5.7 (end); **5.8**
6	Ch. 5 Review and Projects

STARTING OPTIONS

____ Homework Check (5.7): TE page 253; Answer Transparencies
____ Homework Quiz (5.7): TE page 254; Transparencies
____ Warm-Up: Transparencies

TEACHING OPTIONS

____ Notetaking Guide
____ Hands-on Activity: SE pages 255–256
____ Examples: 1–3, SE pages 257–258
____ Extra Examples: TE page 258
____ Your Turn Now Exercises: 1–4, SE pages 257–258
____ Technology Activity with Keystrokes: CRB pages 67–68
____ Concept Check: TE page 258
____ Getting Ready to Practice Exercises: 1–7, SE page 259

APPLY/HOMEWORK

Homework Assignment

____ Block Schedule: pp. 259–261 Exs. 10–22, 24–34 (with 5.7)

Reteaching the Lesson

____ Practice: CRB pages 69–71 (Level A, Level B, Level C); Practice Workbook
____ Study Guide: CRB pages 72–73; Spanish Study Guide

Extending the Lesson

____ Challenge: SE page 260; CRB page 74

ASSESSMENT OPTIONS

____ Daily Quiz (5.8): TE page 261 or Transparencies
____ Test-Taking Practice: SE page 261
____ Quiz (5.5–5.8): SE page 263; Assessment Book page 58

Notes ____

____

____

LESSON 5.8

Name ______________________________ Date __________

Technology Activity

For use with pages 255–261

GOAL Use a spreadsheet to order data.

EXAMPLE **You can order data using a spreadsheet program's *sort* command.**

For one week, 18 of your classmates record the number of hours they spend watching television. You enter the data in the first column of a spreadsheet. Use the spreadsheet to order the data. Then find the median, mode(s), and range of the data.

Original data

	A
1	11.5
2	10.5
3	9.8
4	10.4
5	9.4
6	8.2
7	8.4
8	14.4
9	14.8
10	12.3
11	15.2
12	14.1
13	16.1
14	9.1
15	16.3
16	14.1
17	6.6
18	15.1

Data reordered from least to greatest

	A
1	6.6
2	8.2
3	8.4
4	9.1
5	9.4
6	9.8
7	10.4
8	10.5
9	11.5
10	12.3
11	14.1
12	14.1
13	14.4
14	14.8
15	15.1
16	15.2
17	16.1
18	16.3

Solution

1. Enter the data in the first column.
2. Highlight the data in cells A1:A18.
3. Use the spreadsheet program's sort command to order the data from least to greatest.

Answer: Using the ordered data, it is easier to find the median, mode, and range.

Median: $(11.5 + 12.3) \div 2 = 11.9$

Mode: The mode is 14.1.

Range: Range $= 16.3 - 6.6 = 9.7$

Your turn now **Use a spreadsheet program to order the data. Then find the median, mode(s), and range of the data.**

1. 13, 15, 14, 16, 12, 9, 15, 20, 14, 28, 13, 21, 11, 18, 15, 16, 10, 14, 12, 18
2. 30, 18, 27, 33, 18, 23, 25, 29, 23, 27, 32, 17, 23, 26, 19
3. Hours per week spent studying by twenty-five 12-year olds: 0.6, 5.9, 4.4, 2.4, 6.3, 1.3, 0.2, 4.7, 1, 2.1, 1.8, 4.1, 0.7, 3.8, 8.7, 4.8, 3.4, 7.1, 5.7, 5.4, 4.8, 6, 5, 7.6, 5.9
4. Hours per week spent sleeping by twenty-one 12-year olds: 67.7, 73.5, 68.7, 65.8, 72.7, 75.9, 55.2, 60.3, 57, 67.5, 69.3, 65.4, 60.1, 66, 71.3, 75.9, 59.5, 70.9, 63, 62.9, 68.2

Lesson 5.8

Name ______________________________ Date __________

Technology Activity Keystrokes

For use with Technology Activity, CRB page 67

Excel

Select cell A1 and enter the following.

11.5 ENTER 10.5 ENTER 9.8 ENTER 10.4 ENTER 9.4 ENTER 8.2 ENTER 8.4 ENTER 14.4 ENTER 14.8 ENTER 12.3 ENTER 15.2 ENTER 14.1 ENTER 16.1 ENTER 9.1 ENTER 16.3 ENTER 14.1 ENTER 6.6 ENTER 15.1

Select cells A1:A18. Choose **Sort**... from the **Data** menu. Under **Sort by**, choose Column A and Ascending. Click **OK**.

LESSON 5.8

Name ______________________________ Date __________

Practice A

For use with pages 255–261

In Exercises 1–4, match the term to its value for the following data set. 5, 10, 12, 6, 5, 9, and 2

1. mean | **A.** 5
2. median | **B.** 6
3. mode | **C.** 7
4. range | **D.** 10

In Exercises 5–10, find the mean, median, mode(s), and range of the data.

5. 4, 12, 8, 23, 17, 19, 8

6. −24, −26, −32, −48, −52, −46, −24

7. Numbers of hours worked in a week: 40, 38, 36, 36, 43, 41

8. Basketball points scored: 123, 84, 63, 72, 104, 97, 80

9. Waist measurements: 32, 34, 28, 38, 36, 34, 32, 26, 37

10. Ages of family members: 2, 2, 6, 15, 38, 39

11. The number of tropical cyclones each year from 1992-2000 is shown in the table below. Find the mean, median, and mode(s) of the data. Which average do you think best represents the number of tropical cyclones per year? (Round your answers to the nearest tenth.)

Year	1992	1993	1994	1995	1996	1997	1998	1999	2000
Number of Storms	7	8	7	19	13	8	14	12	15

12. The table shows the number of students that attend some universities and colleges. Find the mean, median, mode(s), and range of the numbers of students enrolled at these schools.

University	Number of Students
Amherst College	1600
Wesleyan University	2700
Vassar College	2400
Bucknell University	3550
DePauw University	2202
Willamette University	1669

13. You recorded the high temperatures for 5 straight days. You know that the average high temperature was 85°F. The temperatures on four of the five days were 80°F, 73°F, 92°F, and 91°F. Determine the high temperature on the fifth day.

LESSON 5.8

Name ____ Date __________

Practice B

For use with pages 255–261

In Exercises 1–6, find the mean, median, mode(s), and range of the data.

1. $-21, -6, -15, -49, -52, -6, -26$

2. 104, 98, 73, 16, 29, 83, 66

3. Bowling scores: 114, 136, 220, 245, 179, 150

4. Numbers of cars over a bridge in an hour: 24, 74, 83, 51, 43, 92, 76, 77

5. Numbers of people per family: 7, 4, 3, 2, 6, 4, 5, 2, 3, 4

6. Wages per hour: \$7.25, \$8.50, \$6.50, \$7.75, \$10

7. The numbers of stories of some tall buildings in Detroit, Michigan, are listed in the table. Find the mean, median, and mode(s) of the number of stories. (Round your answers to the nearest tenth.)

Building	Number of Stories
One Detroit Center	50
Buhl Building	26
Fisher Building	28
Ford Building	19
David Stott Building	37
David Broderick Tower	34

8. The table shows the number of yards several wide receivers gained during their first two football games. Find the mean, median, mode(s), and range of the number of yards gained. Which average do you think best represents the number of yards gained by these receivers over the two games? Explain. (Round your answers to the nearest hundredth.)

Wide Receiver	Number of Yards
Price	265
Mason	227
Moulds	198
Morgan	193
Smith	187
Ward	182
Harrison	178

9. Brian recorded the amount of money he spent over the last 5 days. He knows that the average amount of money he spent was \$25.72. On four of the five days, Brian spent \$15.50, \$28.41, \$31.02, and \$10.66. Determine how much Brian spent on the fifth day.

10. Find the mean of $5x$, $2x$, $7x$, $-2x$, $-4x$, $7x$, and $-x$.

Lesson 5.8

LESSON 5.8

Name ______________________________ Date __________

Practice C

For use with pages 255–261

In Exercises 1–6, find the mean, median, mode(s), and range of data.

1. 17, 15, 11, 19, 16, 12

2. $-105, -56, -87, -91, -56, -74, -77$

3. Laps run: 26, 4, 19, 14, 16, 7, 21, 16

4. Meals eaten at home in a week: 6, 2, 7, 14, 3, 12, 9, 4, 15

5. Prices of hotel rooms in Orlando, FL:
$139, $249, $79, $129, $109, $119, $119, $99, $279

6. Atomic masses of elements:
12.011, 10.81, 114.82, 257, 1.0080, 137.34, 261, 208.98

7. The average radius of each of the nine planets is given in the table. Find the mean, median, and mode(s) of the radii of the planets. Determine the average that best represents these numbers. Explain. (Round your answers to the nearest tenth.)

Planet	Mercury	Venus	Earth	Mars	Jupiter	Saturn	Uranus	Neptune	Pluto
Radius (km)	2430	6060	6370	3370	69,900	58,500	23,300	22,100	1500

8. The data set shows the numbers of minutes that 9 people talked on their cell phones in a month. Find the mean, median, mode(s), and range of the numbers of minutes. (Round your answers to the nearest hundredth.)

105, 24, 175, 300, 580, 295, 175, 52, 406

9. Your last 5 test scores were 74, 96, 81, 86, and 79. You want to have an average of 83 for your 6 tests in math class. Determine what your sixth test score must be in order for you to have an average of 83.

10. Find the mean of $3x$, $9x$, $13x$, $-8x$, $-2x$, $-7x$, and $13x$.

11. Make 2 different data sets that have a mean and a median of 10 and a mode of 6.

12. The table shows the amount of precipitation that Yakutat, Arkansas, received in 11 months. Yakutat usually has an average precipitation of 12.60 inches per month through the year. How many inches would it have needed in December to equal that average?

Month	Jan	Feb	Mar	Apr	May	June
Inches of Rain	12.18	10.67	10.72	9.92	9.66	7.30
Month	**July**	**Aug**	**Sept**	**Oct**	**Nov**	**Dec**
Inches of Rain	8.18	11.54	18.65	22.97	14.52	

Lesson 5.8

Name ______________________ Date __________

Study Guide

For use with pages 255–261

GOAL **Describe data sets using mean, median, mode, and range.**

VOCABULARY

The **mean** of a data set is the sum of the values divided by the number of values.

The **median** of a data set is the middle value when the values are written in numerical order. If the data set has an even number of values, the median is the mean of the 2 middle values.

The **mode** of a data set is the value that occurs most often. A data set can have no mode, 1 mode, or more than 1 mode.

The **range** of a data set is the difference of the greatest value and the least value.

EXAMPLE 1 Finding a Mean

Lora found the following prices for sport shirts: \$20, \$26, \$27, \$28, \$21, \$42, \$18, and \$20. Find the mean of the prices.

$$\text{Mean} = \frac{20 + 26 + 27 + 28 + 21 + 42 + 18 + 20}{8} = \frac{202}{8} = 25.25$$

Answer: The mean price of the sport shirts is \$25.25.

Exercises for Example 1

Find the mean of the data.

1. $-5.9, -7.8, -5.9, -9.5, -6.2$

2. $2\frac{3}{4}$ cm, $2\frac{3}{8}$ cm, $2\frac{1}{2}$ cm, 2 cm

EXAMPLE 2 Finding Median, Mode, and Range

Find the median, mode(s), and range of the daily low temperatures in a city for 6 days.

$-12°F, -19°F, -6°F, -16°F, -19°F, -8°F$

Median Rewrite the temperatures in order from coldest to warmest.

$-19°F, -19°F, -16°F, -12°F, -8°F, -6°F$

The data set has an even number of temperatures, so the median is the mean of the 2 middle values, $-16°F$ and $-12°F$.

$$\textbf{Median} = \frac{-16 + (-12)}{2} = -14$$

The median temperature is $-14°F$.

Lesson 5.8

Name ______________________________ Date __________

Study Guide

For use with pages 255–261

Mode The temperature that occurs most often is $-19°F$.

Range Find the difference of the greatest and the least values.
$(-6°F) - (-19°F) = 13°F$

Exercises for Example 2

Find the median, mode(s), and range of the data.

3. 13, 16, 11, 12, 14, 19, 11, 10, 17, 18, 15, 12, 11

4. 30, 31, 33, 36, 38, 31, 33, 35, 35, 31, 35, 38

EXAMPLE 3 Choosing a Representative Average

The number of raisins in a half dozen cookies from 2 bakeries is given. Which average best describes the number of raisins in a cookie from each bakery?

Bakery 1

20, 17, 18, 19, 14, 18

Bakery 2

5, 12, 23, 23, 8, 15

Solution

Bakery 1

Mean $= \frac{106}{6} \approx 17.7$

Median: 18

Mode: 18

Bakery 2

Mean $= \frac{86}{6} \approx 14.3$

Median: $\frac{12 + 15}{2} = 13.5$

Mode: 23

The mean, median, and mode are very close in Bakery 1. Each represents the data well.

The mean and median in Bakery 2 are close; however, the mode is high. The mean or median represents the data well.

Exercise for Example 3

Find the average that best represents the data.

5. 3, 3, 4, 4, 4, 6, 7, 8, 15, 16

Name ______________________ Date __________

Challenge Practice

For use with pages 255–261

In Exercises 1–3, use the bar graph that shows the lengths of words found in a passage from a novel for adolescents.

1. Find the mode(s). Explain how you found your answer.
2. Find the mean. Round your answer to the nearest whole number. Explain how you found your answer.
3. Find the median. Explain how you found your answer.

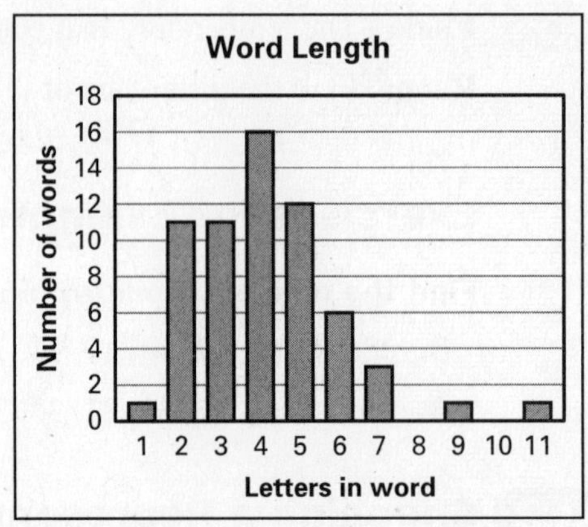

In Exercises 4–7, give an example of a set of six numbers that has the given characteristics.

4. The mode is greater than both the mean and median.
5. The mean is greater than the mode.
6. The mean, median, and mode have the same value.
7. The median is greater than the mean.

In Exercises, 8–10, find the value of the variable(s) in the set of data that satisfies the given condition(s). The data in Exercise 10 are ordered.

8. 7, 4, 3, 2, 8, 5, a, 3
   Range = 7
9. 91, 95, b, 97, 93, 95
   Mean = 95
10. 34, 41, 45, c, 49, 54, d (ordered list of data)
    Median = 46
    Mean = 47

Lesson 5.8

Name ______________________ Date __________

Chapter Review Games and Activities

For use after Chapter 5

Math Bingo

Use your answer to get a bingo. Choose and solve any one of the 20 problems. Look for your answer on the Math Bingo card. If it's there, place an X over it. When you have 4 X's in a row, horizontally, diagonally or vertically, you have a Math Bingo! For more fun, play with a partner. Whoever gets a bingo first is the winner!

M	A	T	H
1	-6.38	$-\frac{1}{3}$	-0.79
2	$-\frac{29}{40}$	2.81	50
-83.21	19	$9\frac{5}{8}$	$\frac{4}{5}$
13.48	16	$-5\frac{2}{7}$	$\frac{1}{6}$

1. $\frac{1}{5} + \frac{2}{5} =$ ____

2. $-4\frac{1}{7} + \frac{3}{7} =$ ____

3. $\frac{1}{6} - \frac{5}{6} + \frac{2}{6} =$ ____

4. $3\frac{3}{4} + \left(-5\frac{1}{5}\right) =$ ____

5. $-\frac{3}{5} - \frac{1}{8} =$ ____

6. $-\frac{2}{3} \cdot \left(-\frac{1}{4}\right) =$ ____

7. $9 \cdot \left(-2\frac{1}{10}\right) =$ ____

8. $\frac{4}{17} \div 3 =$ ____

9. $2\frac{2}{7} \div \left(-\frac{1}{2}\right) =$ ____

10. $\frac{3}{4}x = 12$

11. $\frac{5}{8}y = \frac{1}{2}$

12. $10.7 + 2.78 =$ ____

13. $11.32 - 8.51 =$ ____

14. $-4.07 - 2.31 =$ ____

15. $-12 \div (-0.24) =$ ____

16. $15.7 \cdot (-5.3) =$ ____

In Exercises 17–20, use the following data. –8, 7, 5, –10, –3, 9, –9, 5

17. Find the mean.

18. Find the median.

19. Find the mode.

20. Find the range.

Review and Projects

CHAPTER 5

Name ______________________________ Date __________

Real-Life Project: Making a Quilt

For use after Chapter 5

Objective **Design a quilt and calculate the total cost of making the quilt.**

Materials pencil, paper

Investigation *Getting Going* Suppose you are going to make a quilt using the design and materials shown below. There are three parts to the quilt—the central pattern, the border, and the back. The central pattern is made of twelve 8 inch × 8 inch squares of material. The border is made of four strips of material that are $4\frac{1}{2}$ inches wide. The back is made of a single piece of material that covers the entire back of the quilt to the edges of the border.

Before purchasing the material, you need to calculate the size of each piece. To allow for seams when sewing any two pieces together, you will need to add $\frac{1}{4}$ inch of material onto each seamed side of each piece of material.

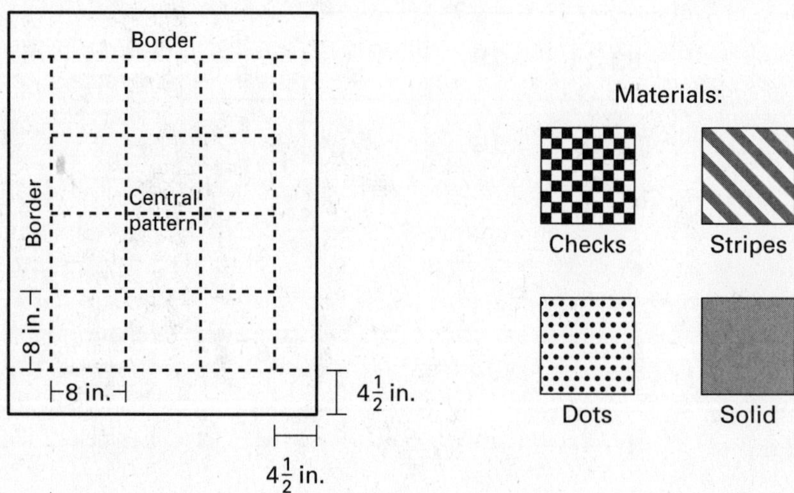

Each of the materials is sold on a bolt. You can buy the length of material you need by the yard in increments of $\frac{1}{4}$ yard. The width of each bolt is 45 inches.

1. Make a sketch of your quilt using the design above and your choice of materials. Determine the total number of yards of each material that you will need to buy. Then determine the total cost of the quilt using the price list at the right.

2. Make your own design for a quilt. Use the Internet, a local fabric store, or another reliable source to find the materials for your quilt. Sketch a drawing of the quilt, list the prices of the different materials that you will use, determine the total number of yards of each material that you will need to buy, and determine the total cost of the finished quilt.

Checks	\$3.15 per yard
Stripes	\$2.50 per yard
Dots	\$1.89 per yard
Solid	\$1.19 per yard

Teacher's Notes for Making a Quilt Project

For use after Chapter 5

Project Goals

- Add and multiply fractions.
- Add and multiply decimals.

Managing the Project

Guiding Students' Work This project will be most effective if the students' work is checked throughout the project. Students often forget to add the seam allowance into their calculations for material. Also, encourage students not to waste material while calculating the amount necessary to complete the quilt. You might want to have them calculate the amount of money lost due to unused material. Encourage the students to use all four materials for a variety of quilt designs. You may want to suggest making a table to organize all of the information.

Rubric for Project

The following rubric can be used to assess student work.

4 The student makes an accurate and creative sketch of the quilt using the design and materials given for Question 1, and then does the same when designing his/her own for Question 2. The student correctly determines the number of yards of material to buy with a minimal amount of excess material for Questions 1 and 2, and also determines the total cost of the quilt. The student has done an acceptable amount of research and lists the prices of material for Question 2. The work is neat and complete.

3 The student makes an accurate and creative sketch of the quilt using the design and materials given for Question 1, and then does the same when designing his/her own for Question 2. The student determines the number of yards of material to buy, but may have slightly more than a minimal amount of excess material for Questions 1 and 2. The student determines the total cost of the quilt with only a few errors for Questions 1 and 2. The student has done an acceptable amount of research and lists the prices of material for Question 2. The work is neat and complete.

2 The student makes a sketch of the quilt using the design and materials given for Question 1, but the sketch may be slightly inaccurate or lacking creativity. The student creates the sketch for his/her own quilt for Question 2 in a similar manner. The student determines the number of yards of material to buy for Questions 1 and 2, but has made some errors or has a considerable amount of excess material. The student determines the total cost of the quilt for Questions 1 and 2 with some errors. The student has done a fair amount of research and lists the prices of material for Question 2. The work may be a bit sloppy or incomplete.

1 The student makes a sketch of the quilt using the design and materials given for Question 1, but the sketch is inaccurate and/or lacking creativity. The student creates the sketch for his/her own quilt for Question 2 in a similar manner. The student determines the number of yards of material to buy for Questions 1 and 2, but has made a substantial number of errors and/or has a considerable amount of excess material. The student determines the total cost of the quilts for Questions 1 and 2 with errors. The student has not done an acceptable amount of research and/or does not list the prices of material for Question 2. The work is sloppy and incomplete.

CHAPTER 5

Name ______________________________ Date __________

Cooperative Project: Dividing Fractions

For use after Chapter 5

Objective **Make models to find quotients of fractions and display them on a poster.**

Materials construction paper, scissors, glue, markers or crayons, pencil, notebook paper

Investigation *Getting Going* You will create models from construction paper to illustrate the division of fractions. Examples of the two types of models you will make are shown below. Whole number units are modeled with a square. Fractional parts of a unit are modeled with a portion of a square.

Type 1 Dividing by a number smaller than the dividend: $1 \div \frac{1}{2}$

Make paper models of the dividend and divisor. Ask yourself, "How many divisor models fit onto the dividend model?"

1 ÷ $\frac{1}{2}$ = $\frac{1}{2}$ $\frac{1}{2}$

Two $\frac{1}{2}$-models fit onto the 1-model. So, $1 \div \frac{1}{2} = 2$.

$1 \quad \div \quad \frac{1}{2} \quad = \quad 2$

Type 2 Dividing by a number larger than the dividend: $\frac{1}{4} \div 2$

Ask yourself, "What fractional part of the divisor fits onto the dividend?"

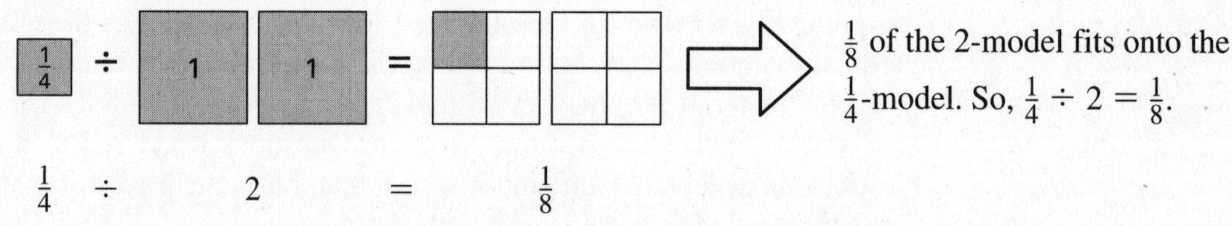

$\frac{1}{8}$ of the 2-model fits onto the $\frac{1}{4}$-model. So, $\frac{1}{4} \div 2 = \frac{1}{8}$.

$\frac{1}{4} \quad \div \quad 2 \quad = \quad \frac{1}{8}$

1. Use models to illustrate the solution of each problem below. Use different colored squares of construction paper to represent the models and glue them to poster board. Use any other materials provided by your teacher to make a total of four creative division posters.

(a) $5 \div \frac{1}{4}$ **(b)** $\frac{1}{8} \div 2$ **(c)** $\frac{1}{2} \div \frac{1}{8}$ **(d)** $\frac{1}{4} \div 1\frac{1}{2}$

2. Use models and make a poster to represent the solutions of the problems $\frac{4}{5} \div \frac{1}{3}$ and $\frac{2}{9} \div \frac{3}{4}$. Explain the additional steps needed to model these solutions.

Teacher's Notes for Dividing Fractions Project

For use after Chapter 5

Project Goals

- Divide fractions.
- Use models to represent division of fractions.
- Use the LCD to make a model for dividing two fractions.

Managing the Project

Classroom Management The groups may include 2-4 students. You may want to give each group a set of fractions different from the ones given in Questions 1 and 2 so that each group has a separate set of fractions to work with.

Guiding Students' Work This is a difficult concept to understand. Stress the importance of choosing whether a problem is of Type 1 or Type 2 before solving the problem. Also stress to your students that whole units should be modeled by squares of uniform size and fractions should be modeled by their corresponding portions of the squares. The students can calculate each problem to check that their posters are correct.

Rubric for Project

The following rubric can be used to assess student work.

4 The students made posters accurately showing the division of all 4 fractions in Question 1. The students attempted and succeeded in making a poster that accurately shows both solutions for the problems in Question 2, and the explanation is accurate with mention of the LCD. The students' models are colored and sized to accurately represent different whole numbers and fractions. The work is neat and complete.

3 The students made posters accurately showing 3 of the divisions in Question 1. The students made a strong attempt to construct a poster that shows the divisions for Question 2, but only 1 of them is correct, and they gave an acceptable application but may not have mentioned the LCD. The students' models are colored and sized to accurately represent different whole numbers and fractions. The work is neat and complete.

2 The students made posters accurately showing 2 of the divisions in Question 1. The students made a strong attempt to construct a poster that shows the divisions for Question 2, but neither is without error, and the explanation may not be complete or has no mention of the LCD. The students' models are colored and sized to acceptably represent different whole numbers and fractions. The work may be slightly sloppy.

1 The students made posters accurately showing 1 of the divisions in Question 1. The students made a weak attempt to construct a poster that shows the divisions from Question 2, and both are incorrect, and the explanation is invalid and has no mention of the LCD. The students' models are not colored and sized to accurately represent different whole numbers and fractions. The work is sloppy or incomplete.

Name ______________________ Date __________

Independent Extra Credit Project: Musical Notation

For use after Chapter 5

Objective **Use time signatures to write measures of music.**

Materials paper, pencil

Investigation In sheet music, notes are written on a *staff* usually made of 5 horizontal lines. Vertical lines divide the staff into *measures*. A piece of music may have any number of measures. The fraction at the beginning of the staff is called the *time signature*. The numerator of the time signature tells how many *beats* there are in a measure. The denominator tells what kind of note makes up a beat. In the time signature below, there are 4 beats in a measure and a *quarter note* has a value of one beat. Likewise, a time signature of $\frac{3}{8}$ tells you there are 3 beats per measure, where the *eighth note* has a value of one beat.

Types of notes

In the staff above, different types of notes are used in each measure. The first measure is made up of 2 *half* notes. The second measure has 4 *quarter* notes. The last measure has 8 *eighth* notes.

1. If a quarter note gets a beat, how many beats does an eighth note get?
2. What kind of note gets a beat in $\frac{6}{8}$ time? How many beats does a half note get? How many beats would 3 *sixteenth* notes get?

Write the number of beats each note gets. Complete the measure with a variety of half notes, quarter notes, or eighth notes.

3. 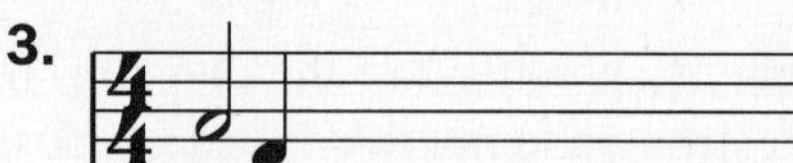

4. 

The symbol ♬ represents 2 sixteenth notes. Write the number of beats each note gets. Complete the measure with a variety of quarter notes, eighth notes, or sixteenth notes.

5. 

6. 

In Exercises 7–10, draw a music staff. Write 4 measures of music in the given time signature. Use half notes, quarter notes, eighth notes, and sixteenth notes. Be sure to put the time signature on the staff.

7. $\frac{3}{4}$ time
8. $\frac{6}{8}$ time
9. $\frac{5}{2}$ time
10. $\frac{5}{4}$ time

Teacher's Notes for Musical Notation Project

For use after Chapter 5

Project Goals

- Add and subtract fractions.
- Multiply fractions.

Managing the Project

Guiding Students' Work As an extension to the project, ask for student volunteers to play or sing the music composed by fellow classmates. You could also have students write more than 4 measures of music for each time signature.

Rubric for Project

The following rubric can be used to assess student work.

4 The student gives the correct number of beats in all the notes asked for. The student accurately completes each measure using a variety of notes. The student writes the required number of measures of music for each time signature. The notes in each measure add up to the correct number of beats, and all the required notes are included.

3 The student gives the correct number of beats in the notes asked for with up to 2 errors. The student completes each measure with notes but may make a mistake or does not use a variety of notes. The student writes the required number of measures of music for each time signature. There may be an incorrect number of beats for the notes written in the measures for 1 of the time signatures, or there may not be all of the required notes in 1 of the time signatures.

2 The student gives the correct number of beats in the notes asked for with up to 4 errors. The student completes each measure with notes but makes more than 2 mistakes or does not use a variety of notes. The student writes the required number of measures of music for each time signature. There may be an incorrect number of beats for the notes written in the measures for 2 of the time signatures. The required notes may not all have been used.

1 The student has more than 4 errors in giving the number of beats in the notes. The student does not complete the measures accurately with notes. The student does not accurately complete the required measures of music for more than 1 time signature.

Name ______________________ Date ________

Cumulative Practice

For use after Chapter 5

Use a calculator to evaluate the expression. (Lesson 1.2)

1. $\frac{15 + 9}{11 - 5}$ **2.** $\frac{21}{0.2 + 1.3}$ **3.** $\frac{13.4 - 2.6}{0.12}$

Write the phrase as a variable expression. Let *x* represent the variable. (Lesson 1.3)

4. the quotient of 14 and a number

5. the sum of a number and 1

6. 11 subtracted from a number

7. 100 times a number

Find the perimeter and area of the rectangle or square. (Lesson 1.6)

8. 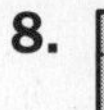

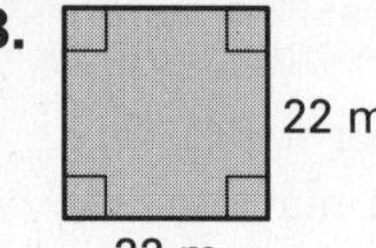

9. 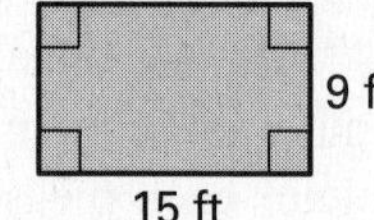

10. 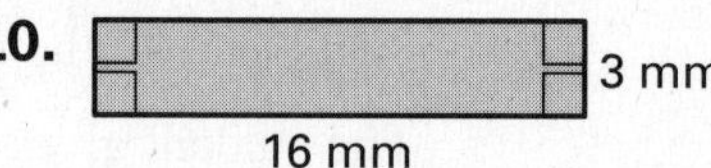

Simplify the expression. (Lesson 2.1)

11. $-(-38)$ **12.** $|-14|$ **13.** $|27|$

14. $-|-10|$ **15.** $-|7|$ **16.** $-[-(-5)]$

Find the sum, difference, product, or quotient. (Lessons 2.2–2.5)

17. $-22 + (-47)$ **18.** $17 + (-3)$ **19.** $-4 - 9$

20. $12 - 30$ **21.** $-1 - (-1)$ **22.** $-4(-15)$

23. $17(-3)$ **24.** $\frac{28}{-4}$ **25.** $\frac{-108}{-12}$

Simplify the expression by combining like terms. (Lesson 2.7)

26. $3a + 4b - 5 - a$

27. $-5y - 15 - 2x + 5y$

28. $4s + 3s + 2t + 3t - 2$

29. $-13x + 12x - 19y - 12x$

Translate the statement into an equation. Then solve the equation. (Lessons 3.1–3.4)

30. A number increased by 40 is equal to 325.

31. The difference between a number and 16 is 29.

32. The sum of 4 and twice a number is 36.

33. One third of a number decreased by 5 is -12.

34. The product of -7 and a number is 91.

Review and Projects

CHAPTER 5 Continued

Name ______________________ Date __________

Cumulative Practice

For use after Chapter 5

Find the area and perimeter of the triangle. (Lesson 3.5)

35.

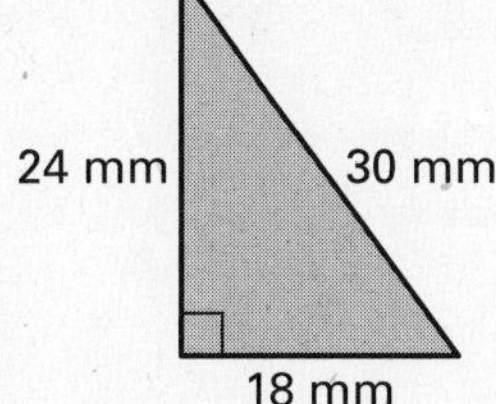

36.

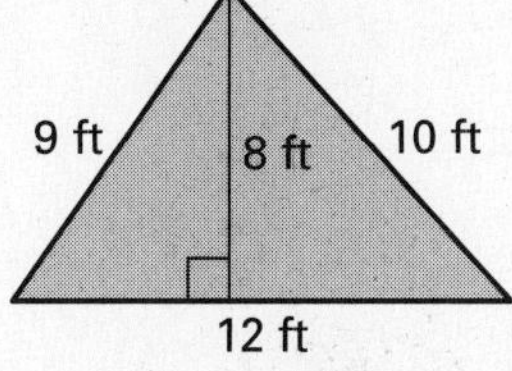

37.

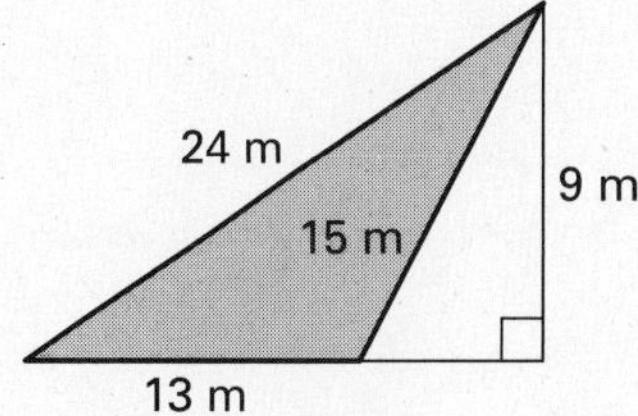

Factor the monomial. (Lesson 4.1)

38. $16ab$ **39.** $75jk^4$ **40.** $100m^2n^3$

Decide whether the numbers are relatively prime. If not, find the greatest common factor. (Lesson 4.2)

41. 40, 77 **42.** 21, 35 **43.** 28, 45

Determine the number that correctly completes the statement. (Lesson 4.6)

44. $10^3 \cdot 10^? = 10^{12}$ **45.** $\frac{9^?}{9^2} = 9$ **46.** $\frac{4^{11}}{4^?} = 4^5$

Write the expression using only positive exponents. (Lesson 4.7)

47. $s^{-4} \cdot s^{-3}$ **48.** $\frac{c^{-1}}{c^7}$ **49.** $\frac{16r^{-6}}{4r^4}$

Write the fraction or mixed number as a decimal. (Lesson 5.5)

50. $\frac{3}{8}$ **51.** $\frac{5}{11}$ **52.** $8\frac{2}{3}$

Write the decimal as a fraction or mixed number. (Lesson 5.5)

53. 0.9 **54.** -0.86 **55.** 0.048

56. -3.5 **57.** $0.\overline{1}$ **58.** $-0.\overline{79}$

Find the mean, median, mode(s), and range of the data. (Lesson 5.8)

59. Points scored in a football season: 149, 146, 176, 164, 161, 144, 145, 147, 155, 145, 150, 145, 149

60. Salaries: \$23,000; \$21,500; \$95,000; \$19,700; \$20,400; \$22,600

61. Test grades: 52%, 88%, 69%, 86%, 75%, 86%

Answers

Lesson 5.1

Practice A

1. $\frac{3}{7}$ **2.** $\frac{1}{3}+\frac{1}{3}=\frac{2}{3}$ **3.** $\frac{2}{3}$ **4.** $\frac{4}{17}$ **5.** $-\frac{2}{5}$ **6.** 3 **7.** $1\frac{11}{21}$ **8.** $2\frac{4}{7}$ **9.** $-2\frac{1}{5}$ **10.** $-10\frac{1}{5}$ **11.** $-13\frac{5}{11}$ **12.** $\frac{2d}{3}$ **13.** $\frac{3x}{5}$ **14.** $\frac{g}{6}$ **15.** $-m$ **16.** $1\frac{4w}{13}$ **17.** $\frac{p}{2}$ **18.** $\frac{1}{2}$ mile **19.** 5 cups **20.** $1\frac{3}{5}$ **21.** $-1\frac{1}{3}$ **22.** $\frac{1}{8}$ **23.** $1\frac{10}{21}$ **24.** $-6\frac{3}{17}$ **25.** $\frac{3}{10}$

Practice B

1. $\frac{7}{8}-\frac{3}{8}=\frac{4}{8}$ or $\frac{1}{2}$ **2.** $\frac{7}{8}$ **3.** $-\frac{1}{3}$ **4.** $\frac{1}{2}$ **5.** $3\frac{1}{2}$ **6.** $-2\frac{2}{5}$ **7.** $\frac{2}{3}$ **8.** $-\frac{2}{3}$ **9.** $-4\frac{1}{2}$ **10.** $3\frac{1}{2}$ **11.** $1\frac{h}{3}$ **12.** $-\frac{x}{5y}$ **13.** $-\frac{v}{w}$ **14.** $\frac{3}{4}$ pound **15.** $6\frac{5}{6}$ hours **16.** $\frac{13}{14}$ **17.** $-\frac{1}{2}$ **18.** $-\frac{1}{3}$ **19.** $-\frac{7}{18}$ **20.** $-6\frac{3}{4}$ **21.** $2\frac{11}{12}$ **22.** $x=\frac{2}{3}$ **23.** $w=\frac{2}{5}$ **24.** $b=1\frac{1}{4}$

Practice C

1. $1\frac{2}{5}$ **2.** $-\frac{4}{7}$ **3.** $\frac{2}{7}$ **4.** $3\frac{2}{3}$ **5.** $-\frac{1}{4}$ **6.** $2\frac{3}{7}$ **7.** $-5\frac{1}{9}$ **8.** $-7\frac{6}{23}$ **9.** $-7\frac{1}{5}$ **10.** $1\frac{a}{3}$ **11.** $\frac{3m}{5n}$ **12.** $-\frac{11g}{12h}$ **13.** $7\frac{1}{5}$ hours **14.** $\$4\frac{1}{2}$ **15.** $1\frac{8}{15}$ **16.** $-1\frac{4}{15}$ **17.** $\frac{1}{6}$ **18.** $-\frac{3}{8}$ **19.** $-\frac{3}{10}$ **20.** $1\frac{1}{28}$ **21.** $-1\frac{11}{19}$ **22.** $3\frac{1}{20}$ **23.** $-\frac{3}{26}$ **24.** $a=\frac{2}{5}$ **25.** $p=\frac{7}{12}$ **26.** $p=1\frac{2}{13}$ **27.** $\frac{7}{12}$ **28.** $\frac{1}{8}$ **29.** $\frac{12}{13}$

Study Guide

1. $\frac{8}{11}$ **2.** $1\frac{1}{5}$ **3.** $1\frac{5}{7}$ **4.** $\frac{a}{9}$ **5.** $\frac{3}{8y}$ **6.** $\frac{6x}{7}$ **7.** $5\frac{2}{3}$ in. **8.** $\frac{5}{9}$ **9.** $\frac{11}{12}$ **10.** $3\frac{3}{8}$

Challenge Practice

1. 1 **2.** 19 **3.** -3 **4.** -1 **5.** 2 **6.** -13

7. The subtraction sign should distribute through both the x and the 8.

$$\frac{x-5}{x}-\frac{x+8}{x}=\frac{x-5-x-8}{x}=\frac{-13}{x}$$

8. $3\frac{7}{8}$ ft **9.** $3\frac{6}{7}$ m

Lesson 5.2

Practice A

1. 8 **2.** 30 **3.** 21 **4.** 48 **5.** D **6.** B **7.** A **8.** C **9.** $\frac{1}{4}$ **10.** $1\frac{1}{12}$ **11.** $1\frac{5}{12}$ **12.** $-\frac{17}{40}$ **13.** $\frac{13}{60}$ **14.** $-\frac{1}{24}$ **15.** $2\frac{2}{3}$ **16.** $-\frac{5}{7}$ **17.** $8\frac{11}{120}$

18. Hours 1st day + Hours 2nd day + Hours 3rd day = Total hours

19. $7\frac{1}{8}+4\frac{5}{9}+h=20$ **20.** $8\frac{23}{72}$ hours **21.** true **22.** true **23.** false **24.** $\frac{8h}{15}$ **25.** $2\frac{13x}{21}$ **26.** $\frac{3+8y}{12y}$ **27.** $1\frac{29}{48w}$

Practice B

1. $\frac{5}{8}$ **2.** $\frac{77}{90}$ **3.** $1\frac{37}{65}$ **4.** $-\frac{31}{88}$ **5.** $-\frac{1}{140}$ **6.** $-1\frac{2}{5}$ **7.** $4\frac{5}{42}$ **8.** $9\frac{5}{21}$ **9.** $4\frac{83}{104}$ **10.** $11\frac{11}{40}$ **11.** $11\frac{107}{120}$ **12.** $11\frac{13}{24}$ **13.** Stephanie **14.** $5\frac{7}{24}$ pies **15.** false **16.** true **17.** false **18.** $-\frac{16x}{45}$ **19.** $-\frac{m}{55}$ **20.** $\frac{70+26p}{91p}$ **21.** $1\frac{79}{168q}$ **22.** $x=2\frac{1}{2}$ **23.** $y=3\frac{5}{6}$ **24.** $w=2\frac{13}{16}$ **25.** $4\frac{7}{8}$ yards

Practice C

1. $\frac{1}{10}$ **2.** $1\frac{11}{48}$ **3.** $1\frac{157}{600}$ **4.** $\frac{1}{84}$ **5.** $-\frac{83}{180}$ **6.** $3\frac{49}{52}$ **7.** $-\frac{21}{23}$ **8.** $5\frac{57}{104}$ **9.** $7\frac{45}{77}$ **10.** yes **11.** no **12.** false **13.** true **14.** false **15.** $\frac{13x}{342}$ **16.** $\frac{372a+322}{713}$ **17.** $\frac{191}{210f}$ **18.** $c=2\frac{4}{5}$ **19.** $b=2\frac{1}{18}$ **20.** $a=4\frac{3}{5}$ **21.** $\frac{6}{25}$ meter

Study Guide

1. $\frac{25}{15}$ **2.** $-\frac{3}{20}$ **3.** $\frac{c}{14}$ **4.** $-\frac{18x}{35y}$ **5.** $3\frac{1}{2}$ qt

Real-World Problem Solving

1. $\frac{1}{12}$ h **2.** $\frac{3}{20}$ h **3.** 10 minutes over **4.** A: $\frac{13}{60}$ h, B: $\frac{7}{60}$ h, C: $\frac{1}{6}$ h, D: $\frac{1}{6}$ h, E: $\frac{2}{15}$ h

Lesson 5.2 *continued*

Challenge Practice

1. $-\frac{137}{432}$ **2.** $-\frac{983}{38,416}$ **3.** $3\frac{1}{2}$ **4.** $-4\frac{9}{40}$ **5.** $49\frac{47}{48}$ in. **6.** yes **7.** $\frac{11}{16}$ in. remains **8.** $\frac{3}{40}$ **9.** $\frac{3}{10}$

Lesson 5.3

Activity Master

1. $\frac{3}{20}$ **2.** $\frac{15}{30}$ **3.** $\frac{3}{14}$ **4.** $\frac{4}{27}$ **5.** *Sample Answer:* The product of two fractions can be written as the product of the numerators divided by the product of the denominators.

Practice A

1. c; b **2.** improper fractions **3.** C **4.** A **5.** D **6.** B **7.** $\frac{12}{35}$ **8.** $\frac{15}{52}$ **9.** $\frac{7}{22}$ **10.** -1 **11.** $8\frac{2}{5}$ **12.** 10 **13.** $8\frac{7}{16}$ **14.** -30 **15.** $9\frac{5}{8}$ **16.** $\frac{2}{7}$ **17.** $\frac{8}{45}$ **18.** $-1\frac{25}{63}$ **19.** 3 **20.** 9 cups **21.** $16\frac{1}{3}$ ft^2 **22.** $1\frac{2}{25}$ in.^{2}

Practice B

1. $\frac{1}{20}$ **2.** $\frac{8}{27}$ **3.** $\frac{9}{20}$ **4.** -1 **5.** 12 **6.** $10\frac{1}{2}$ **7.** $30\frac{13}{45}$ **8.** $-27\frac{1}{7}$ **9.** $29\frac{3}{5}$ **10.** $\frac{7}{18}$ **11.** $\frac{33}{52}$ **12.** $-\frac{77}{120}$ **13.** $2\frac{13}{32}$ **14.** $1555\frac{1}{2}$ m^2 **15.** $2\frac{4}{25}$ m^2 **16.** $168\frac{2}{7}$ in.^{2} **17.** $71\frac{91}{99}$ cm^2 **18.** $-\frac{14}{135}$ **19.** -6 **20.** $7\frac{13}{28}$ **21.** $\frac{91}{225}$

Practice C

1. $\frac{9}{16}$ **2.** $\frac{5}{12}$ **3.** $\frac{14}{15}$ **4.** -1 **5.** $9\frac{3}{4}$ **6.** $11\frac{2}{3}$ **7.** $27\frac{35}{36}$ **8.** $-57\frac{1}{7}$ **9.** -154 **10.** $\frac{11}{50}$ **11.** $\frac{14}{25}$ **12.** $-\frac{66}{125}$ **13.** $-1\frac{179}{195}$ **14.** $665\frac{7}{25}$ m^2 **15.** $16\frac{7}{15}$ m^2 **16.** $55\frac{23}{135}$ yd^2 **17.** $-\frac{11}{162}$ **18.** $-12\frac{48}{91}$ **19.** $6\frac{881}{1134}$ **20.** $1\frac{212}{225}$ **21.** $\frac{7}{80}$ **22.** $6\frac{527}{576}$ **23.** $3\frac{3557}{5000}$ oz

Study Guide

1. $\frac{24}{5}$ **2.** $-\frac{4}{9}$ **3.** $-\frac{1}{4}$ **4.** $\frac{3}{10}$ **5.** $2\frac{21}{32}$ **6.** $-15\frac{3}{4}$ **7.** $4\frac{1}{5}$ **8.** $9\frac{23}{35}$ **9.** $-\frac{2}{9}$ **10.** $\frac{1}{18}$ **11.** $-\frac{8}{243}$ **12.** $\frac{1}{81}$

Challenge Practice

1. $-\frac{37}{672}$ **2.** $-\frac{1037}{2310}$ **3.** $4192\frac{151}{160}$ **4.** $-27\frac{17}{21}$ **5.** $9\frac{2}{7} \cdot 3\frac{3}{4} = \frac{65}{7} \cdot \frac{15}{4} = \frac{975}{28} = 34\frac{23}{28}$; $(9 \cdot 3)\left(\frac{2}{7}\right)\left(\frac{3}{4}\right) = 5\frac{11}{14}$; $34\frac{23}{28} \neq 5\frac{11}{14}$ **6.** $\frac{a}{b} \cdot \frac{Ce + d}{e} = \frac{a(Ce + d)}{be} = \frac{aCe + ad}{be}$

Lesson 5.4

Practice A

1. $3 \div \frac{3}{8}$; 8 **2.** $\frac{9}{7}$ **3.** -11 **4.** $\frac{1}{6}$ **5.** $-\frac{5}{14}$ **6.** 10 **7.** $-3\frac{3}{14}$ **8.** $-\frac{80}{119}$ **9.** $-1\frac{106}{125}$ **10.** $\frac{1}{18}$ **11.** $-\frac{1}{18}$ **12.** $2\frac{2}{3}$ **13.** $-2\frac{25}{27}$ **14.** $-1\frac{23}{93}$ **15.** $1\frac{9}{28}$ **16.** $-\frac{14}{15}$ **17.** $1\frac{6}{7}$ **18.** $x = 27$ **19.** $y = 10$ **20.** $w = -24$

21. Number of pies = Number of guests × Serving size **22.** $12 = g \times \frac{1}{8}$ **23.** 96 guests

24. $12\frac{1}{7}$ servings.

Practice B

1. $\frac{17}{3}$ **2.** $-\frac{22}{7}$ **3.** $\frac{1}{12}$ **4.** $\frac{10}{39}$ **5.** $\frac{2}{7}$ **6.** $-\frac{4}{15}$ **7.** $\frac{98}{165}$ **8.** $-1\frac{29}{192}$ **9.** $\frac{3}{26}$ **10.** $-\frac{1}{22}$ **11.** $1\frac{23}{32}$ **12.** $-\frac{329}{402}$ **13.** $2\frac{1}{102}$ **14.** $-\frac{57}{80}$ **15.** $\frac{51}{98}$ **16.** $-4\frac{103}{119}$ **17.** $a = 16$ **18.** $b = -30$ **19.** $w = 91$ **20.** 6 **21.** $10\frac{1}{6}$ pieces **22.** 10 **23.** $\frac{5}{14}$ **24.** -20 **25.** $98\frac{3}{10}$ yd

Practice C

1. No; reciprocals have the same sign. **2.** $1\frac{13}{27}$ **3.** $-1\frac{25}{96}$ **4.** $-1\frac{1}{25}$ **5.** $-1\frac{1}{9}$ **6.** $\frac{1}{70}$ **7.** $-\frac{5}{121}$ **8.** $3\frac{1}{21}$ **9.** $-\frac{63}{130}$ **10.** $2\frac{13}{15}$ **11.** $-\frac{13}{27}$ **12.** $\frac{7}{22}$ **13.** $-4\frac{4}{63}$ **14.** $g = 78$ **15.** $h = -8\frac{1}{3}$ **16.** $j = 40$

17. $9\frac{49}{164}$ shingles **18.** 364; 273 divided by $\frac{3}{4}$ **19.** 2 **20.** 1 **21.** $-5\frac{17}{20}$ **22.** *Sample Answer*: Find the area of the board and the area of one square and divide.; 64 squares

Study Guide

1. $\frac{10}{9}$ **2.** $-\frac{22}{21}$ **3.** $\frac{4}{3}$ **4.** $\frac{15}{8}$ **5.** $-\frac{1}{36}$ **6.** $\frac{1}{28}$ **7.** $-\frac{1}{40}$ **8.** $-\frac{1}{56}$ **9.** $9\frac{1}{2}$ **10.** $\frac{2}{3}$ **11.** -2 **12.** $1\frac{1}{2}$ **13.** 40 days

Challenge Practice

1. 0; Division by 0 is undefined. **2.** *Sample Answer*: 8 **3.** *Sample Answer*: $\frac{1}{4}$ **4.** *Sample Answer*: $-\frac{3}{4}$ **5.** *Sample Answer*: $-\frac{3}{2}$ **6.** 1 and -1 **7.** ac **8.** $\frac{8x^3}{y^3}$ **9.** $\frac{80y^2}{3x^2}$ **10.** $\frac{15c^2b}{2}$

Lesson 5.5

Practice A

1. integers; zero **2.** remainder **3.** repeating **4.** whole number, integer, rational number **5.** rational number **6.** integer, rational number **7.** rational number **8.** -0.4 **9.** $0.1\overline{6}$ **10.** 0.46 **11.** $-0.41\overline{6}$ **12.** 0.4375 **13.** -2.5 **14.** $4.5\overline{3}$ **15.** $3.\overline{7}$ **16.** $-0.\overline{69}$ **17.** $0.6\overline{81}$ **18.** -9.9 **19.** $-0.9\overline{5}$ **20.** $\frac{18}{25}$ **21.** $-\frac{9}{20}$ **22.** $1\frac{7}{25}$ **23.** $2\frac{13}{20}$ **24.** $-\frac{41}{300}$ **25.** $-\frac{3}{5}$ **26.** $\frac{67}{999}$ **27.** $\frac{284}{999}$ **28.** 0.2, $\frac{1}{4}$, $\frac{2}{7}$, 0.3, $\frac{1}{3}$ **29.** $4\frac{3}{4}$, 4.8, $4\frac{7}{8}$, $4\frac{8}{9}$, 4.9 **30.** 15.25, 15.4, 14.88, 16.5, 15.6; 14.88, 15.25, 15.4, 15.6, 16.5

Practice B

1. C **2.** A **3.** B **4.** integer, whole number, rational number **5.** rational number **6.** rational number **7.** integer, rational number **8.** 0.6 **9.** $-0.\overline{4}$ **10.** $-0.\overline{81}$ **11.** 0.6875 **12.** 3.125 **13.** $-5.\overline{148}$ **14.** $7.\overline{48}$ **15.** 0.825 **16.** -0.07 **17.** 0.5 **18.** -8.38 **19.** $-0.\overline{6930}$ **20.** $\frac{6}{25}$ **21.** $-\frac{61}{100}$ **22.** $2\frac{12}{25}$ **23.** $7\frac{3}{20}$ **24.** $-\frac{1}{3}$ **25.** $\frac{19}{20}$ **26.** $-\frac{124}{999}$ **27.** $-\frac{109}{1000}$ **28.** $\frac{3}{4}$, 0.8, 0.81, $\frac{11}{13}$, $\frac{6}{7}$ **29.** $6\frac{2}{19}$, $6\frac{1}{8}$, 6.15, $6\frac{1}{5}$, 6.3 **30.** Warner: $0.\overline{6}$; Collins: $0.\overline{846153}$; Griese: 0.7; Garcia: 0.75; Favre: $0.65\overline{90}$ **31.** Collins, Garcia, Griese, Favre, Warner

Practice C

1. rational number, integer, whole number **2.** rational number **3.** rational number **4.** rational number, integer **5.** 0.875 **6.** $-0.\overline{90}$ **7.** $-0.3\overline{48}$ **8.** 0.34375 **9.** 0.56 **10.** $3.41\overline{6}$ **11.** $7.31\overline{6}$ **12.** -8.75 **13.** $-1.41\overline{6}$ **14.** $-2.7\overline{63}$ **15.** $-0.\overline{756}$ **16.** -0.545 **17.** $\frac{7}{20}$ **18.** $-\frac{14}{25}$ **19.** $1\frac{17}{25}$ **20.** $9\frac{3}{100}$ **21.** $-\frac{7}{9}$ **22.** $\frac{2}{15}$ **23.** $-\frac{7}{11}$ **24.** $-2\frac{49}{200}$ **25.** $\frac{12}{17}$, 0.75, $\frac{19}{25}$, 0.78, $\frac{35}{44}$ **26.** $7\frac{2}{5}$, 7.41, $7\frac{8}{17}$, 7.48, $7\frac{29}{38}$ **27.** $0.\overline{1}$, $0.\overline{2}$, $0.\overline{3}$; $0.\overline{4}$, $0.\overline{7}$ **28.** 0.03, 0.014, 0.012, 0.015, 0.05; swimming, football, basketball, soccer, volleyball **29.** 12 **30.** 16

Study Guide

1. $0.8\overline{3}$ **2.** $0.4\overline{6}$ **3.** $0.\overline{81}$ **4.** 1.1, $1\frac{2}{7}$, 1.3, $1\frac{5}{12}$, $1\frac{1}{2}$ **5.** -0.4, $-\frac{7}{18}$, $-\frac{3}{8}$, -0.3, $-\frac{1}{5}$ **6.** $\frac{3}{4}$ **7.** $4\frac{3}{1000}$ **8.** $-2\frac{9}{25}$ **9.** $\frac{5}{9}$ **10.** $\frac{4}{11}$ **11.** $\frac{19}{99}$

Challenge Practice

1.

Fraction	Decimal
$\frac{1}{7}$	$0.\overline{142857}$
$\frac{2}{7}$	$0.\overline{285714}$
$\frac{3}{7}$	$0.\overline{428571}$
$\frac{4}{7}$	$0.\overline{571428}$
$\frac{5}{7}$	$0.\overline{714285}$
$\frac{6}{7}$	$0.\overline{857142}$

Lesson 5.5 *continued*

2. The digits are in the same order, but the pattern begins at different numbers.

3. $\frac{6}{7} = 6 \times \frac{1}{7} = 6 \times \left(0.\overline{142857}\right) = 0.\overline{857142}$

4. $5 \times \left(0.\overline{076923}\right) = 0.\overline{384615}$

5. $0.\overline{0588235294117647}$

6. $0.\overline{052631578947368421}$

7. $0.\overline{0434782608695652173913}$

8. The maximum is one less than the denominator.

9. *Sample Answer*: $\frac{1}{11} = 0.\overline{09}$, which only has 2 digits, not 10 digits in the repeating pattern.

Lesson 5.6

Practice A

1. B **2.** C **3.** A **4.** D **5.** 20.712 **6.** 3.361 **7.** −6.105 **8.** −1.65 **9.** 6.463 **10.** −12.276 **11.** −5.965 **12.** 43.69 **13.** 15.122 **14.** −6.52 **15.** 20.2 **16.** −1.084 **17.** $w = 38.4$ **18.** $x = 5.53$ **19.** $z = 18.61$ **20.** $a = 0.86$ **21.** $m = -7.33$ **22.** $p = -2.83$ **23.** 31 **24.** 69 **25.** 79 **26.** 117 **27.** \$16.45 **28.** 18.39 ft **29.** 36.18 in. **30.** 29.24 ft **31.** Line up decimal points; 20.963 **32.** 4.75 pounds

Practice B

1. 19.303 **2.** 1.868 **3.** −3.546 **4.** −3.58 **5.** 3.684 **6.** −19.445 **7.** −9.608 **8.** 43.758 **9.** 16.569 **10.** −5.85 **11.** 36.307 **12.** −1.075 **13.** $f = 30.7$ **14.** $g = 7.81$ **15.** $h = 23.01$ **16.** $j = 17.685$ **17.** $k = -1.444$ **18.** $m = -15.072$ **19.** 31 **20.** 64 **21.** 98 **22.** 132 **23.** \$135.25 **24.** 18.38 cm **25.** 34.6 m **26.** 31.48 in. **27.** 100 + 70 + 5 + 0.9 + 0.02 + 0.003 + 0.0001 **28.** 7.125 yd **29.** no **30.** 0.075 yd

Practice C

1. 28.456 **2.** 2.302 **3.** −6.526 **4.** −4.505 **5.** 17.623 **6.** −9.564 **7.** 43.94 **8.** 14.169 **9.** −10.54 **10.** −7.35 **11.** 32.416 **12.** −1.083 **13.** $a = 19.19$ **14.** $b = 24.31$ **15.** $c = = 4.933$ **16.** $d = 6.33$ **17.** $e = 9.328$ **18.** $f = -3.276$ **19.** 41 **20.** 109 **21.** 82 **22.** 34 **23.** 33.141 mm **24.** 29.891 in. **25.** 2000 + 900 + 80 + 4 + 0.5 + 0.07 + 0.001 + 0.0003 **26.** 10.94 **27.** −0.58 **28.** 13.69 **29.** 2.608 **30.** 17.95 miles **31.** Madison; write the fraction as a decimal to compare.

Study Guide

1. −19.22 **2.** 9.181 **3.** 1.559 **4.** 3.629 **5.** 2.6 **6.** 24.17 **7.** 36 **8.** 8.11 **9.** \$25 **10.** 80

Real-World Problem Solving

1. \$3.75 **2.** \$1.75 **3.** \$2.00 **4.** $\$3.75 + x = \$10.00$; \$6.25

Challenge Practice

1. −54.96 **2.** −6.285 **3.** −14.116 **4.** −32.143 **5.** 0.5 **6.** $0.\overline{22}$ **7.** $0.\overline{796}$ **8.** $-0.\overline{78}$ **9.** $-0.\overline{725543}$ **10.** $-0.\overline{45} - 0.\overline{3} = -\frac{45}{99} - \frac{3}{9} = -\frac{5}{11} - \frac{1}{3} = \frac{-15}{33} - \frac{11}{33} = \frac{-26}{33} = -0.\overline{78}$

Lesson 5.7

Practice A

1. product; factors **2.** leading digit **3.** A **4.** C **5.** B **6.** 6 **7.** 17.08 **8.** −0.95 **9.** 8 **10.** 120 **11.** −45.1 **12.** −91.8175 **13.** 1.5 **14.** 4.0898 **15.** 17.54 **16.** 0.1468535 **17.** 36.2 **18.** Area = length × width **19.** Area = 28.7 × 15.3; 439.11 m^2 **20.** 15 × 29 = 435 **21.** 14.95 g **22.** 13 **23.** 6.5 **24.** 17.557 **25.** −0.7332 **26.** −14.39 **27.** 41.7231

Practice B

1. C **2.** B **3.** A **4.** 2.56 **5.** 67.34 **6.** −1.792 **7.** 9 **8.** 24.5 **9.** −28.15 **10.** −173.3418 **11.** 3.87 **12.** 14.25 **13.** 0.89 **14.** 0.0114 **15.** 7.4 **16.** Area = length × width **17.** A = 0.305 × 0.305; 0.093025 km^2 **18.** 0.3 × 0.3 = 0.09 **19.** 6.234375 **20.** 0.9 **21.** 15.906 **22.** −0.06966 **23.** −25.44

Lesson 5.6 *continued*

24. 23.6898 **25.** 21.5 patties **26.** 22.75 in.^{2} **27.** −2.91 **28.** 4 **29.** 37.73 **30.** \$3.59

Practice C

1. 2.52 **2.** 10.27 **3.** −16.445 **4.** 3.8008 **5.** 0.067925 **6.** 5.4 **7.** $20.\overline{6}$ **8.** $54.8\overline{3}$ **9.** −5.4 **10.** −126.676992 **11.** 12.56 **12.** 6.85 **13.** 25 stamps **14.** 34 boards **15.** 52; 62 more **16.** 8.24 **17.** −15.38 **18.** 58.8693 **19.** 44.31 **20.** 7.5 **21.** 30.73

Study Guide

1. −28.395 **2.** 109.8027 **3.** −8.91 **4.** 0.115 **5.** 3.1 **6.** 1.15 **7.** 1.4 **8.** 2.35 **9.** 0.15625 **10.** 0.208

Challenge Practice

1. 55.0314 m^2 **2.** 84.9056 in.^{2} **3.** 405.702 ft^2 **4.** 609.930012 cm^2 **5.** 7.4 mm **6.** 12.4 in.

Lesson 5.8

Technology Activity

1. median: 14.5; modes: 14 and 15; range: 19

2. median: 25; mode: 23; range: 16

3. median: 4.7; modes 4.8 and 5.9; range 8.5

4. median: 67.5; mode: 75.9; range: 20.7

Practice A

1. C **2.** B **3.** A **4.** D **5.** mean: 13; median: 12; mode: 8; range: 19 **6.** mean: −36; median: −32; mode: −24; range: 28 **7.** mean: 39; median: 39; mode: 36; range: 7 **8.** mean: 89; median: 84; mode: no mode; range: 60 **9.** mean: 33; median: 34; modes: 32, 34; range: 12

10. mean: 17; median: 10.5; mode: 2; range: 37 **11.** mean: 11.4; median: 12; modes: 7, 8; Best average: answers will vary. **12.** mean: 2353.5; median: 2301; no mode; range: 1950 **13.** 89°F

Practice B

1. mean: −25; median: −21; mode: −6; range: 46 **2.** mean: 67; median:73; no mode; range: 88 **3.** mean: 174; median: 164.5; no mode; range: 131 **4.** mean: 65; median: 75; no mode; range: 68 **5.** mean: 4; median: 4; mode: 4; range: 5 **6.** mean: 8; median: 7.75; no mode; range: 3.5 **7.** mean: 32.3; median: 31; no mode; range: 31 **8.** mean: 204.29; median: 193; no mode; range: 87; Best average: median, because 4 of the 7 were at or below this number. **9.** \$43.01 **10.** $2x$

Practice C

1. mean: 15; median: 15.5; no mode; range: 8

2. mean: −78; median: −77; mode: −56; range: 49 **3.** mean: 15.375; median: 16; mode: 16; range: 22 **4.** mean: 8; median: 7; no mode; range: 13

5. mean: \$146.78; median: \$119; mode: \$119; range: \$200 **6.** mean: 125.37; median: 126.08; no mode; range: 259.992 **7.** mean: 21,503.33; median: 6370; no mode; range: 68,400; Best average: answers may vary. **8.** mean: 234.67; median: 175; mode: 175; range: 556 **9.** 82 **10.** $3x$ **11.** *Sample Answer*: Set 1: 6, 6, 14, 14 and Set 2: 6, 6, 6, 10, 14, 14, 14 **12.** 14.89 in.

Study Guide

1. −7.06 **2.** $2\frac{13}{32}$ cm **3.** median: 13; mode: 11; range: 9 **4.** median: 34; modes: 35 and 31; range: 8 **5.** mean: 7; median: 5; mode: 4; the median and mode best describe the data values.

Challenge Practice

1. 4-letter words; The highest bar in the graph represents the most frequent word length.

2. 4-letter words; Find the total number of letters in the passage and divide by the number of words in the passage.

3. 4-letter words; Locate the middle number of the 62 words in the graph. **4.** *Sample Answer*: 1, 2, 3, 4, 5, 5 **5.** *Sample Answer*: 1, 1, 1, 1, 1, 10

6. *Sample Answer*: 0, 1, 5, 5, 9, 10 **7.** *Sample Answer*: 0, 1, 6, 6, 7, 8 **8.** $a = 1$ or 9 **9.** $b = 99$ **10.** $c = 46, d = 60$

Review and Projects

Chapter Review Games and Activities

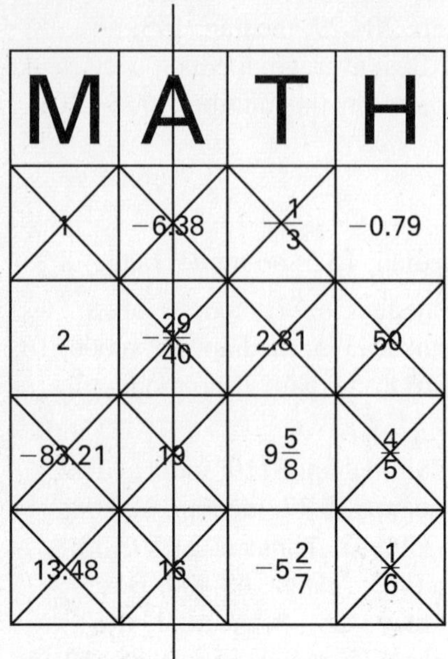

1. $\frac{3}{5}$ **2.** $-3\frac{5}{7}$ **3.** $-\frac{1}{3}$ **4.** $-1\frac{9}{20}$ **5.** $-\frac{29}{40}$ **6.** $\frac{1}{6}$ **7.** $-18\frac{9}{10}$ **8.** $\frac{4}{51}$ **9.** $-4\frac{4}{7}$ **10.** $x = 16$ **11.** $y = \frac{4}{5}$ **12.** 13.48 **13.** 2.81 **14.** −6.38 **15.** 50 **16.** −83.21 **17.** mean: −0.5 **18.** median: 1 **19.** mode: 5 **20.** range: 19

Real-Life Project

1. Check students' work. **2.** Check students' work.

Cooperative Project

1. (a) 20 (b) $\frac{1}{16}$ (c) 4 (d) $\frac{1}{6}$ **2.** $\frac{12}{5}$; $\frac{8}{27}$; Explanations will vary.

Independent Extra Credit Project

1. $\frac{1}{2}$ **2.** eighth note; 4; $1\frac{1}{2}$ **3.** 2 beats; 1 beat; Check notes drawn by students. **4.** $\frac{1}{2}$ beat; $\frac{1}{2}$ beat; Check notes drawn by students. **5.** 2 beats; $\frac{1}{4}$ beat; $\frac{1}{4}$ beat; $\frac{1}{2}$ beat; Check notes drawn by students. **6.** $\frac{1}{4}$ beat; $\frac{1}{4}$ beat; $\frac{1}{2}$ beat; Check notes drawn by students.

7–10. Check student drawings.

Cumulative Practice

1. 4 **2.** 14 **3.** 90 **4.** $14 \div x$ **5.** $x + 1$ **6.** $x - 11$ **7.** $100x$ **8.** $P = 88$ m; $A = 484$ m^2 **9.** $P = 48$ ft; $A = 135$ ft^2 **10.** $P = 38$ mm; $A = 48$ mm^2 **11.** 38 **12.** 14 **13.** 27 **14.** −10 **15.** −7 **16.** −5 **17.** −69 **18.** 14 **19.** −13 **20.** −18 **21.** 0 **22.** 60 **23.** −51 **24.** −7 **25.** 9 **26.** $2a + 4b - 5$ **27.** $-2x - 15$ **28.** $7s + 5t - 2$ **29.** $-13x - 19y$ **30.** $n + 40 = 325$; 285 **31.** $n - 16 = 29$; 45 **32.** $4 + 2n = 36$; 16 **33.** $\frac{1}{3}n - 5 = -12$; −21 **34.** $-7n = 91$; −13 **35.** $A = 216$ mm^2; $P = 72$ mm **36.** $A = 48$ ft^2; $P = 31$ ft **37.** $A = 58.5$ m^2; $P = 52$ m **38.** $2 \cdot 2 \cdot 2 \cdot 2 \cdot a \cdot b$ **39.** $3 \cdot 5 \cdot 5 \cdot j \cdot k \cdot k \cdot k \cdot k$ **40.** $2 \cdot 2 \cdot 5 \cdot 5 \cdot m \cdot m \cdot n \cdot n \cdot n$ **41.** relatively prime **42.** 7 **43.** relatively prime **44.** 9 **45.** 3 **46.** 6 **47.** $\frac{1}{s^7}$ **48.** $\frac{1}{c^8}$ **49.** $\frac{4}{r^{10}}$ **50.** 0.375 **51.** $0.\overline{45}$ **52.** $8.\overline{6}$ **53.** $\frac{9}{10}$ **54.** $-\frac{43}{50}$ **55.** $\frac{6}{125}$ **56.** $-3\frac{1}{2}$ **57.** $\frac{1}{9}$ **58.** $-\frac{79}{99}$ **59.** mean: 152; median: 149; mode: 145; range: 32 **60.** mean: \$33,700; median: \$22,050; no mode; range: \$75,300 **61.** mean: 76%; median: 80.5%; mode: 86%; range: 36%